THE COMPLETE GUIDE TO
MAKE $100,000
A YEAR AS A BARBER

**LEARN THE SECRETS AND TECHNIQUES THAT
CAN TURN YOU INTO A MONEY MAKING MACHINE**

ALLEN BROWN
AKA MASTER BARBER AL

BUILD OUR KINGDOM PUBLISHING
—— BUILD OUR KINGDOM.COM ——

The Complete Guide To Make $100,000 A Year As A Barber
Copyright © 2024 by Build Our Kingdom Publishing, LLC and
Allen Brown
Published by Build Our Kingdom Publishing, LLC

Printed in the United States of America
1st Edition December 2024 First Printing

ISBN for paperback: 978-1-964203-08-9

Build Our Kingdom Publishing, LLC. 560 Main St, Stroudsburg, PA 18360

Edited by: Allen Brown

Although the publisher and the author have made every effort to ensure that the information in this book was correct at press time and while this publication is designed to provide accurate information in regard to the subject matter covered, the publisher and the author assume no responsibility for errors, inaccuracies, omissions, or any other inconsistencies herein and hereby disclaim any liability to any party for any loss, damage, or disruption caused by errors or omissions, whether such errors or omissions result from negligence, accident, or any other cause.

This publication is meant as a source of valuable information for the reader, however, it is not meant as a substitute for direct expert assistance. If such a level of assistance is required, the services of a competent professional should be sought.

Table of Contents

Table of Contents iii

Dedication vii

Acknowledgement...viii

Introduction Making $100,000 a Year as a Barber................................ 1

Chapter 1 My $100,000 Barbering Journey..5

Chapter 2 The Six-Figure Barber Career Foundation........................... 13

Chapter 3 Skills That Pay the Bills: Mastering Your Craft 21

Chapter 4 Charge What You're Worth: Getting Top Dollar! 27

Chapter 5 Your Ticket to Wealth: Building a Loyal Clientele 33

Chapter 6 7 Proven Ways to Pack Your Chair with Customers 39

Chapter 7 The Must-Have Barber Skills That Keep Clients Coming 47

Chapter 8 Customer Service Hacks to Boost Your Earnings................. 53

Chapter 9 How Barbershop Culture Drives Profits 59

Chapter 10 What Gets You More Cash: Booth Rent vs. Commission ... 65

Chapter 11 Location, Location, Cash Flow Picking the Right Spot 71

Chapter 12 Hiring Barbers Who Help You Make More Money........... 75

Chapter 13 The 3 Business Skills Every Money-Making Barber Needs 81

Chapter 14 Big Goals, Big Money: Setting Your Barbering Targets 85

Chapter 15 Rent or Own? The Barbershop Decision That Changes Ev . 89

Chapter 16 Negotiating Like a Boss: The Deal That Sets You Up......... 95

Chapter 17 How to Raise Money for Your Own Barbershop.............. 101

Chapter 18 30 Game-Changing Tips for Barber Success 107

Chapter 19 Making Money Beyond the Barbershop 115

Chapter 20 Safety First: Protecting and Profits 123

Chapter 21 Keep More Cash – Pay Less Taxes: Business Structure & 127

Phase 2 How I Built a Six-Figure Barbershop in Two Years 134

Phase Two Introduction:100K Barber Shop in Less Than Two Years 135

Blueprint 1 Why I Jumped Back into the Game 139

Blueprint 2 Scouting the Competition and Winning 143

Blueprint 3 Finding the Goldmine Location 147

Blueprint 4 Making the Landlord Work for You 151

Blueprint 5 Don't Break the Bank Setting Up Shop 155

Blueprint 6 My Launch Plan for a Packed Barbershop 159

Blueprint 7 Pricing Strategies That Maximize Your Profits 163

Blueprint 8 Setting Big Goals for Your Barbershop's Success 167

Blueprint 9 Attracting Barbers Who Fit Your Vision 171

Blueprint 10 The Real Booth Rent vs. Commission Strategy 175

Blueprint 11 Writing Ironclad Barber Agreements 179

Blueprint 12 Appointments vs. Walk-ins: The Business Model That .. 183

Blueprint 13 Managing Your Shop Like a True Professional 187

Blueprint 14 Managing Online Reviews – Turning Negatives into Po 191

Blueprint 14 Handling Online Reviews – Part 2 195

BarberShopCashFlow.com 199

About Allen Brown 203

About Build Our Kingdom Publishing 205

DON'T STOP HERE!

Visit **BarberShopCashFlow.com**
and get your lifetime membership access!

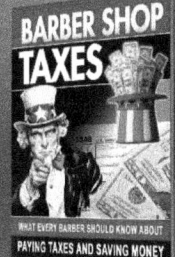

Dedication

I dedicate this book to myself—for the dedication and focus I've put in since the age of 14. From owning three barbershops and a barber school to working toward the ultimate goal of owning my own building with a barbershop in it, these have been my greatest accomplishments.

I appreciate all the mentors who have dropped valuable nuggets of wisdom along the way, and I am deeply grateful to God for giving me the strength to pursue my dreams and keep moving forward.

This book is dedicated to my journey and perseverance.

Master Barber Al

Acknowledgement

First and foremost, I want to give a special shout-out to all the barbers who came up in the game with me. You all helped sharpen my skills and contributed to my growth. Jonathan Brown, Marlon Baily, Sam H., Buddha, Rome Gee, Junior the Barber, Ty Lewis, Tyrone M., Sateek G., Troy V., Rob Jones (Flex Razor Owner), Nat (My Barber Pops and the person who signed my apprentice papers), and my brother Todd Brown—each of you played a vital role in my career, and I can honestly say I wouldn't be one of the best in the game without your influence.

I want to acknowledge Marty, who was the first to put me in a barbershop at the age of 15. Respect!

To all the other barbers I came up with, I see you, and I appreciate you. The time we spent together in the shop shaped me into the person I am today.

Peace and blessings to all my brothers, and everyone who shared those unforgettable moments in the barbershop. We had a lot of great times, and those memories will always stay with me.

I also want to acknowledge the Pocono Barbers crew. Jeep Rabinowitz, Isaiah Brown, Matt Gallagher, Micaiah Brown, Josiah Brown, and Jayden DuBose. Keep it pushing. Much success to all of you!

Introduction
Making $100,000 a Year as a Barber

So, you want to make $100,000 a year in the barber business? Well, this is the book you definitely want to read. My name is Allen Brown, also known as Master Barber Al, and I've been doing my thing for over 35 years. I first stepped into the game at the age of 14. A few years later (1993), at the age of 18, I opened my first

barbershop, Brown Brothers. After that, I opened my second barbershop at the age of 22 after meeting my wife (Short Cuts in 1997). I made even more strides in the business after that time. I can honestly say I have been very successful in the barber game, and I have a lot of information that I want to share with you in this book.

I've seen the ups and downs, witnessed some barbers make it, and seen others fail. There's a special level of dedication needed if you want to be successful in the barber business. I wrote this book to share the wisdom I've gained over the years.

Owning my first barbershop at the age of 18 wasn't something I planned. It was a leap of faith. I had to take a chance, and it paid off. That first barbershop came to me unexpectedly, but I was ready for the challenge, and I had that shop for several years. I made a lot

of money there, and I want to share that experience with you, as well as provide insights to help you open your own shop if you desire to one day.

While this book focuses on my journey, I want to be clear: you don't have to own a barbershop to make $100,000 a year. But since I've owned several shops and a barber school, I'll speak a lot from that perspective. However, I want you to know that ownership offers you the opportunity to make even more money while giving you leverage over your time.

Throughout this book, I'll be dropping nuggets on how I built my businesses. The barbershops I built were very successful, and I believe this will help you avoid many of the pitfalls that barbers commonly fall into.

Now, let me share how this book is broken down so you can understand it. In 2016, I decided to create a course for barbers. It was December 2016, and I had been out of the shop for over 10 years. But I had been making a lot of money online, so I decided to create a course to show barbers what I did from the early 90s to the early 2000s. As I put this course together, I was reinspired to open my third barbershop, and by 2019, I hit the $100,000 mark comfortably every year.

Master Barber Al

The first phase of the book explores my life from age 14 through the opening of my second shop. In this phase, I'll share lessons about building your clientele, managing money, and other key aspects of the business. The second phase begins in 2017 when I opened my third barbershop. It walks you through the blueprint of what I did when I returned to the business and grew my shop quickly to surpass $100,000 annually. Some of the information will be repeated from phase one, but it's almost like two different books: one showing you how I did it in my earlier years and one showing you how I successfully relaunched my business after a 10-plus year break.

At the time of this writing in 2024, that third shop is still in operation, now run by my sons, who began cutting hair in 2018 and 2019. I was able to make my dream come true by owning the building that my barbershop is located in. I'll talk about that in the second phase, and you'll see how I went from renting space to owning a building that houses my barbershop, with two storefronts and 11 apartments. This part of my journey is very important to me, especially because I wasted a lot of money on rent during my early years. As I got older, I became wiser and made better decisions. When I rented my third location, I negotiated a right of first refusal in case the owner wanted to sell the building, and that is exactly how I purchased the building. I'll share those details with you as well.

This is how I was able to set goals and build up so that I can eventually retire with multiple streams of income, even after I retire from the barber business. Many barbers don't consider what they'll do after their barbering days are over, but I address that in this book.

One thing I can promise is that this book will provide you with valuable information straight from my own experiences. Some of the information may already be out there, but this is my unique story, and I believe it's extremely valuable to you.

I'm confident that this book will offer a wealth of insight to help you grow your barber business into something successful.

So, let's get into it.

Chapter 1
My $100,000 Barbering Journey

MY JOURNEY

I can't say exactly when I got the bug to become a barber. I do know I was inspired by a good friend of mine named Jonathan Brown, who started cutting hair in the neighborhood. But even before that, I can remember going to the barbershop with my father and enjoying the experience. My younger brother, Todd, who is also a barber and owns a barber school and previously owned several shops, would also come with me.

We were young boys then, and I vividly recall those visits. My father would tell the barber to cut all my hair off—no fancy styles, just a clean, even cut. Even though my brother and I would talk about the styles we wanted on the way to the shop, once we got in the chair, my father made the final call, "cut it all off" he would say. Still, I enjoyed every moment of the experience. I loved looking at the barber's clippers and feeling the comfort of the vibrations as they ran over my head.

I never owned a pair of clippers growing up, but my first real desire to make money with them started when Jonathan was cutting my hair. At some point, he left the neighborhood to attend barber school, leaving a void for everyone who still wanted haircuts. That's when, at the age of 13, I picked up my first pair of clippers and began cutting my own hair and my brother's.

THE FIRST CLIPPERS

I remember going to the store with my father, asking him for money to buy clippers. It was around the time I was 13 or 14 years old, and I had spotted a pair of Oster clippers at a beauty supply store for $14.99. My pops told me to do a couple of chores, and with the money I earned, I bought them. That moment marked a big change in my life.

These clippers weren't fancy—they had no fader or trimmer. But I began experimenting with them. I would take the clippers and make lines around the head, not fading them out, just creating something different from the standard cuts we got at the barbershop. My brother and I ended up with bowl haircuts and straight lines, but we thought we looked sharp. Sometimes, we would add S-curls or flat tops to the mix. Looking back, I'm sure it looked ridiculous, but to me, it was the start of something amazing.

THE BEDROOM BARBERSHOP

I can remember setting up a small barbershop in my bedroom. I hung my clippers on a hook, grabbed a mirror, and invited friends from the neighborhood over for $5 haircuts. It was simple, but it was one of my first real taste of entrepreneurship.

THE GAME-CHANGER: UPGRADING MY TOOLS

I started to develop my craft, even with just that one pair of clippers. One day visiting my aunt's salon in Brooklyn I noticed she had an Andis Outliner clipper that she rarely used, and every time I went there, I would beg her to let me have it. It was about the third visit when she finally gave it to me. That was my first pair of professional clippers, and they changed everything. I was now able to create sharp lines and edge-ups at the end of my haircuts.

FROM THE BASEMENT TO BIGGER DREAMS

With the Andis Outliner in hand, I got serious about cutting hair. Kids from the neighborhood started coming to my basement, where my parents allowed me to set up a barbershop. Little did I know, this was the beginning of a journey that would finance much of my life.

JANUARY 2020

I TOOK A RIDE TO QUEENS NY TO LOCATE MARTY

THIS IS THE GUY THAT HIRED ME AT 15 YEARS OLD
TO WORK IN HIS BARBERSHOP IN 1990
HE ALSO FIRED MY BROTHER...LOL

What started as a hobby when I was 13 and 14 years old grew into something much larger. By the time I turned 50, I had owned three barbershops, established my own barber school, purchased real estate, and started other businesses. Over the years, I've made millions of dollars—all starting from the Oster clipper I decided to buy for $14.99 when I was a teenager.

Barbering has not only been a good move for me—it has been the foundation for everything I've achieved.

THE VISION OF SUCCESS AS A BARBER

As the years went on, by the time I was 14 or 15, I landed my first job at a barbershop. My friend Marlon, who started cutting hair a little after me, excelled much faster than I did. He was able to connect with some local barbers, which eventually landed him in one of the most popular barbershops in Queens, New York. Knowing this, I pushed myself to get better so I could ask Marlon to put me on at the same spot.

Marlon told me to let him know when I was ready, and I took that to heart. After about six more months of cutting hair, honing my craft, and even taking on some of Marlon's overflow clients, I felt confident. Cutting so much hair made me improve quickly—practice really does make perfect. I finally asked Marlon to help me get a chair at the barbershop. He told me to stop by, but when I was ready to meet the boss, I could never find him. Marlon was nowhere to be found when I needed him, so I decided to take matters into my own hands.

I went directly to the owner of the shop, a man named Marty and introduced myself. Without hesitation, Marty told me, "Get your clippers, and you can start tomorrow." I was excited—nervous, but excited. That moment came on a Sunday, which was typically the slowest day in the shop. For new barbers, it was an opportunity to prove themselves to the owner without the pressure of a full crowd.

This was 1989, and at that time, there was no YouTube or social media to learn from. Everything I knew came from hands-on practice in the neighborhood. By the time 1990 rolled around, I was ready. I took the leap, started working at the shop, and never looked back.

BUILDING SUCCESS IN THE SHOP

I developed quickly as a barber, building a massive clientele. The progress was fast, and honestly, a little scary. I was making $500 to $700 a week as a 15-year-old. Back then, haircuts were much cheaper—if you got $15 from a client, that was a big deal, and $20 meant they were getting the royal treatment. But even with those rates, I was earning enough to buy jewelry, my first car, and just about anything I wanted.

Master Barber Al

As my skills improved and my clientele grew, an opportunity to own my own shop opened up. I have to admit, at 18 years old, I didn't have a clear vision of what that meant for my future—it just sort of unfolded. I was doing what I loved, enjoying my freedom, and when the opportunity presented itself, I decided to take the leap.

TAKING THE LEAP TO OWNERSHIP

Here's what happened: A customer who frequented the shop I worked at had opened his own barbershop with another barber. Unfortunately, the other barber went to jail, leaving the customer to run the shop alone. He hired a few other barbers, but they stole from him, leaving him in a bad position. He was about to lose the shop, so he came to talk to the manager at my shop, hoping someone would take it over.

The manager asked the other barbers if anyone wanted to take the opportunity, but none of them were interested. There were seven barbers in the shop, and they all turned it down. That's when I thought, "Maybe this is for me." I wasn't happy where I was, so I decided to step out on faith and say yes.

The shop was just four or five blocks away from my original one. To keep this short, the owner of the shop defaulted on the rent. The landlord came to me asking for his money. I was shocked to find out the rent was only $1,400 a month—I had been handing over way more than that to the current owner. I told the landlord I could handle it, and that's how I got my first barbershop.

THE VISION BECOMES CLEAR

At just 18 years old, I became my own boss. I had other barbers working for me, and I was running my own barbershop. I didn't even have my barber's license at the time! I received my barber license the following year.

I want to emphasize this: It took a little bit of faith, a little bit of education, and a whole lot of consistency for the vision to unfold. Owning my first shop made everything much clearer. If you truly want to succeed as a barber, the most important thing is to start— start whenever and however you can.

Tips to Take Action Now

TIP 1: DON'T BE AFRAID TO EXPLORE NEW OPPORTUNITIES

Opportunities will come your way, but you must be ready to step out on faith and take them. Even if you're unsure, stepping into something new can be the start of something great—just like my first barbershop at 18 years old.

Start Now: Be open to opportunities around you. Whether it's taking a chair at a new shop, trying a new technique, or even considering ownership, trust yourself to take the leap. Write down any opportunities you've hesitated to pursue and make a plan to act on them.

TIP 2: STUDY THE BEST AND MAKE IT YOUR OWN

The best barbers are always learning. Watch the top barbers around you, pick up on what they do well, and incorporate it into your style. Then, add your own flair to make it uniquely yours.

Start Now: Spend time observing skilled barbers in your area. Pay attention to their techniques and how they interact with clients. Practice what you learn on your own clients and refine it until it feels natural.

TIP 3: BUILD YOUR SKILLS THROUGH PRACTICE

Honing your craft is essential to your growth. The more you cut, the better you'll get, and the more confidence you'll have.

Start Now: Set aside time each week to practice cuts, even if it's just on family or friends. Push yourself to master the basics, like smooth fades and sharp lines, and don't be afraid to try something new to expand your skills.

TIP 4: TAKE EVERY CUT SERIOUSLY

Every haircut is a chance to improve your skills and grow your reputation. Whether it's a paying customer or a friend, treat every cut as if it's your most important one.

Start Now: Focus on giving each client your best effort. Make sure every haircut you do represents your brand. Pay attention to detail, and finish strong with a sharp hairline or clean edge-up that leaves a lasting impression.

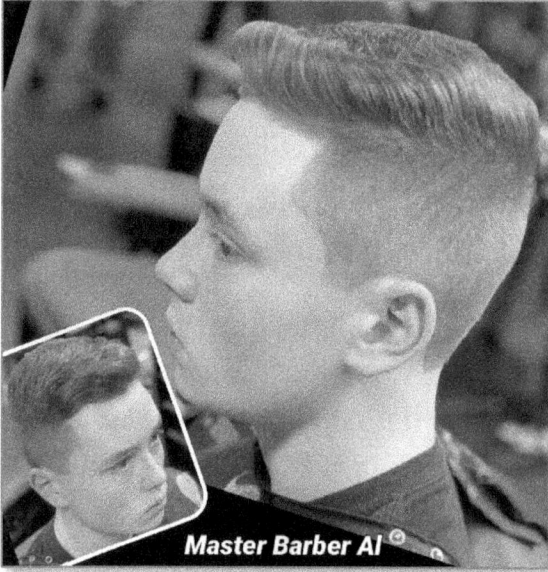

Master Barber Al

HOW TO START TAKING ACTION TODAY

The first step to building your success is putting in the work now. Study the barbers you admire, take what you learn, and practice until your skills are undeniable. Don't shy away from opportunities, even if they seem intimidating—step out on faith and make the most of them. With consistent effort and a willingness to learn, you'll lay the foundation for a career that can take you anywhere.

Chapter 2
The Six-Figure Barber Career Foundation

This book is broken into two phases. The first phase focuses on building your individual clientele and establishing your skills as a barber, while the second phase dives into the process of owning your own shop and growing that clientele to meet financial goals. I've experienced both sides of the business—first, working to build my personal clientele, and later, running barbershops and mentoring others.

Even before I owned my first barbershop at 18, I had already been cutting hair for years, starting in the neighborhood and eventually in a barbershop at just 15. I had to learn a lot along the way. Although I was already business-minded from the way I started, working in a shop required me to level up. I had to focus on professionalism, how to represent myself, and how to work alongside other barbers.

Master Barber Al

SETTING THE STAGE FOR SUCCESS

Back in the '90s, cutting hair alone didn't make you $100,000 a year—not easily, anyway. I'm not even sure if anyone could pull in six figures just cutting hair back then. But today, with the prices we can charge and the opportunities available, a dedicated barber can easily make $100,000 a year.

Here's the math: If you're making $1,800 to $2,000 a week, you'll hit that six-figure mark. Some barbers struggle to even make $1,000 a week, but that shouldn't be the case if you're applying the principles I share in this book. I'm going to show you how to structure your craft and your business to hit those numbers.

One of the most important things is setting clear goals. If you're just cutting hair without a vision or plan, you're not likely to reach your full potential. If you want to use barbering as a tool to finance your life and future endeavors, then this book is for you. I've done it, and I've done it well.

HONING THE CRAFT

Your skill level is critical. Barbering is a craft that develops over time, and back in the day, we didn't have YouTube to teach us. I had to sit behind barbers for hours, just watching how they cut hair. I learned from some of the best in my circle: my boys Sam, Buddha, Rome, and Junior, along with a few others. I'd take a little bit of what I saw each of them do and apply it to my own style.

At that time, I was working in a shop on 161st Street in South Jamaica, Queens. This wasn't just any barbershop—it was the spot where all the major drug dealers in Queens would come to get their cuts. I'm talking about guys from the Supreme Team, 40 Projects, and New York Boulevard (later renamed Guy R. Brewer Boulevard).

If you couldn't hang in this shop, you'd either get clowned or end up in a violent altercation with one of these clients. I'll never forget how nervous I was as a 15-year-old cutting some of the biggest drug dealers in Queens. But once my skills were tight, I didn't worry. A little fear can help you focus. The thought of messing up someone's haircut and facing consequences kept me sharp.

BUTTER ON THE CUTS

Outside of just working, I had a personal drive to be known as one of the best. My boy Buddha gave me the nickname "Butter" because I used to run to the corner store for Buttermilk cookies after every few haircuts. In the hood, nicknames stick quick, and soon, everyone was calling me Butter. Some thought it was because my cuts were smooth, like butter. Either way, the name stuck, and it became part of my brand.

By the time I was standing on my feet all day cutting hair on

Master Barber Al

Fridays and Saturdays, people were calling the shop asking for me specifically. "Yo, is Butter there? What time is Butter coming in?" Clients were waiting outside or calling me to find out their spot in line. It became addictive. I was blowing up.

Walking down Jamaica Avenue, people would recognize me and call out, "Yo, what up, Butter!" It was clear I had built a massive clientele. But that didn't just happen—it came from my desire to be the best. I wanted my fades to be the sharpest and my haircuts to be the cleanest. I wanted people to see my work and think, "Damn, that's crisp."

EARNING RESPECT

I'll never forget one day in the shop when I was cutting a walk-in client. A guy named Dog, from 40 Projects, was sitting with the boss watching me cut. Dog had never been in my chair before, but when I finished, he was just staring at the haircut. He looked at me and said, "Yo, that haircut is crazy."

The client got up, handed me $30, and said, "That's the best haircut I've ever gotten." That moment was huge for me. I had worked hard to get there, and when people started paying premium prices and recognizing my skills, I knew I had made it.

It was all about enhancing my craft and striving to be the best, no matter what it took. That's the kind of focus and drive you need if you want to succeed as a barber.

IT'S YOUR BRAND

Part of getting your whole brand popping is making a conscious decision to be the best. Once you get your brand properly established, and people know who you are, your name starts to spread. A lot of people want great haircuts, and once everybody knows you're the one who's delivering, your reputation builds.

Getting those crispy cuts—that's the first step. You have to hone your skills to the point where you're giving haircuts so sharp that people can't help but take notice. Now, these days, they might call it something different than "crispy," but that's the terminology we used back in the day, so I'm sticking with it. You know what I mean. Maybe before that, people might've called it a "sharp haircut."

What I'm trying to tell you is this: You've got to have such a strong desire to get your skills to the highest level that everybody wants to sit in your chair—even other barbers' customers. Now, I know barbering can be competitive. Sometimes it's friendly, and sometimes it's not. But you want people to desire to sit in your chair so badly that your reputation makes them come to you.

When those clients leave your shop, they're walking billboards and they are telling everyone where they received that cut. That's the best marketing in barbering—*even to this day*—word of mouth.

A TIP TO TRACK YOUR PROGRESS

Here's a tip: Every time you get a new customer, ask them how they found out about you. Specifically, if they asked for you by name, find out what led them to you. This helps you track what's working or even see what people are saying about you.

For me, that's happened so many times. I'll get a request from a new client, and when I ask how they heard about me, the stories always surprise me. A lot of times, it's from strangers who've seen my work. They'll say, "I was walking through Walmart, and I saw this guy's haircut. It was a real tight fade. I asked him, 'Yo, who faded you like that?' and he told me about you."

That's what word of mouth looks like. Your work is your representation. The people showing off your cuts are the ones building your clientele. Many times, new clients come in, and it's because someone saw one of my cuts and couldn't help but ask about it.

It could even be a woman sending her man to you because she wants him to look sharp. The point is, you've got to understand that every cut you do is like an advertisement for your skills.

FOCUS ON BUILDING YOUR SKILLS

I'm going to get deeper into these concepts later in this book, but I just wanted to scratch the surface here. You need to make sure your skills are on point and where they need to be for you to hit the income level you're aiming for.

It all starts with the quality of your cuts. That's your foundation, and it's what will take you where you want to go in this business.

Tips to Take Action Now

TIP 1: BUILD YOUR SKILLS TO STAND OUT

Your skill level is the foundation of your success. The sharper your skills, the more clients will seek you out. Word of mouth starts with the quality of your work, so focus on giving every client the best haircut you can.

Start Now: Identify areas where your skills could improve. Are your fades smooth? Are your lines sharp? Practice on friends or mannequins, and pay attention to every detail. Make sure your cuts are consistently "walking billboards" for your talent.

TIP 2: DELIVER TOP-NOTCH CUSTOMER SERVICE

Clients remember how you treat them just as much as the haircut you give them. Be punctual, respect their time, and always deliver the style they ask for. Excellent customer service builds loyalty and encourages clients to recommend you to others.

Start Now: Take stock of how you handle appointments and client interactions. Are you always on time? Are you focused during their cut? Commit to improving any weak spots in how you serve your clients, starting with being reliable and attentive.

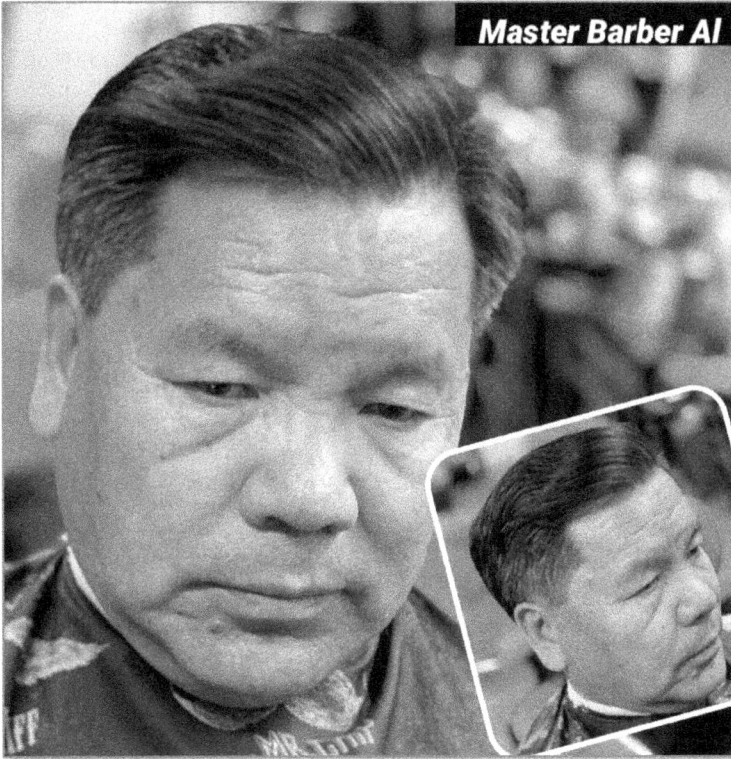
Master Barber Al

TIP 3: TURN EVERY CLIENT INTO A MARKETING OPPORTUNITY

Every client is a chance to grow your brand. When you cut someone's hair, you're not just giving them a style—you're creating an advertisement for your skills.

Start Now: Ask each new client how they found you, and track the answers to see what's working. Encourage satisfied customers to recommend you to their friends. When someone asks where they got their haircut, make sure your name is the first thing they say.

HOW TO START TAKING ACTION TODAY

To put these tips into practice, focus on your cuts and your clients. Sharpen your skills so that every haircut stands out and attracts new customers. Work on building relationships with your clients by treating them with professionalism and respect. The combination of great haircuts and great service will set you apart and help you grow your business starting today.

Chapter 3
Skills That Pay the Bills: Mastering Your Craft

I briefly touched on the importance of having skills as a barber in the last chapter to really build up your clientele. But now, I want to dive a little deeper into what you should really focus on as a barber—not just in this time, but in general. It's an old saying, but it's one I live by: **"Skills pay the bills."**

MASTERING ESSENTIAL CUTS

When I was growing up in the late '80s and '90s, there were a few cuts you absolutely *had* to master. These were the bread-and-butter cuts that could make or break your reputation:

- **Dark Caesar with waves**: This was one of the most popular cuts, and you had to do it perfectly.
- **A flawless fade**: You needed to create a smooth transition from dark to light, or light to dark, without leaving any lines. The fade had to look natural, with no visible transitions.
- **Half-moon parts**: A clean and precise half-moon part could set you apart as a barber.
- **Flat tops**: While less common now, flat tops were a staple back then, and you had to be able to execute them.

Everything else was easier, like a light Caesar, which is a haircut that's pretty simple once you get the technique. To be honest, if you only did Caesars and built a clientele around them, you could still make good money as a barber. But the key is to be versatile. The more you can offer, the more clients you'll attract.

SHARP LINES MAKE ALL THE DIFFERENCE

After you finish any haircut, the finishing touch is sharpening up the hairline with a straight-edge razor. Where I grew up, and even now, a sharp hairline is the ultimate representation of a great haircut. Sometimes the fade might not be 100%, but if the hairline isn't sharp, it can ruin the whole cut. A crisp line is non-negotiable.

ADAPTING TO THE TIMES

Now, in the days we're living in, there are other skills you need to meet the demands of the culture. For example, enhancements have become a big thing. Whether you like it or not, clients often want their hairlines sprayed to make them sharper or to fill in light spots. These enhancements weren't a thing in the '90s, but now you have to adapt if you want to remain competitive.

If you want to focus on a specific clientele or style, that's cool too—you can still be effective. But expanding your skill set gives you more opportunities and increases your earning potential.

CUSTOMER SERVICE SKILLS

Another crucial skill you need to develop is **customer service**. I've seen barbers lose business—sometimes to me—because they didn't treat their clients well. Here are some common mistakes to avoid:

- Not keeping appointments or running late.
- Taking too long on a haircut.
- Being on your phone while cutting hair.
- Ignoring what the customer wants and doing what *you* think looks good instead.

I've seen barbers leave clients sitting in the chair while they go grab food or take a break. That's one of the most inconsiderate things you can do. Why not schedule your breaks between haircuts? That way, you're not inconveniencing your clients.

I remember watching customers leave and take their business to another barber because of this kind of behavior. And I was one of the barbers who benefitted.

HOW I WON OVER CUSTOMERS

One tip I can give you is to talk to everyone in the shop—even other barbers' customers. Some barbers are territorial and don't want you forming relationships with their clients. But I didn't care. I made it my business to talk to everyone.

Here's why: Clients sometimes might be in a hurry, and the barber they usually go to has a wait or is booked. If that client knows you and has seen your work, they might hop in your chair. That's where you shine…lol!

When those opportunities came, I would always give them my best haircuts. I paid attention to what they usually got from their barber and thought about how I could do it better. Once they were in my chair, I made sure they left thinking it was the best haircut they'd ever had. And trust me, once you impress someone like that, they'll keep coming back—and they'll bring others. It's at this point where you can Joke with the barber you took the customer from…lol!

MOVING EFFICIENTLY

Another thing I learned early on is the importance of moving efficiently. Some barbers take an hour and a half for a single cut. While that's fine for certain clients, most people appreciate speed and precision.

When I was 15 or 16, I could cut a client's hair in 15 minutes, and that speed helped me build my clientele. I'll talk more about the balance between speed and quality later in this book, but for now, remember this: The faster you can move people through while maintaining quality, the more clients you can serve and the more money you can make.

Tips to Take Action Now

TIP 1: FOCUS ON MASTERING ESSENTIAL CUTS

To build a solid reputation as a barber, start by mastering the foundational cuts that everyone wants. Make sure your fades are clean, with no visible lines, and your hairlines are razor-sharp. Pay attention to detail, because these are the skills that will set you apart.

Start Now: Practice the basics relentlessly. Offer discounted or even free cuts to friends and family to refine your technique. Watch how other barbers execute fades, parts, and sharp lines, and replicate what you see until it becomes second nature.

TIP 2: ADAPT TO MODERN TRENDS

Stay up-to-date with what today's clients want. Whether it's enhancements like hairline sprays or special styling techniques, meeting these demands can open new doors for your business.

Start Now: Invest in tools or products that align with current trends. Experiment with enhancements like sprays or powders on your own hair or mannequins. Watch tutorials and practice these techniques to incorporate them into your offerings.

TIP 3: BUILD STRONG CUSTOMER RELATIONSHIPS

Good customer service is just as important as your skills. Treat every client with respect, be on time, and always deliver what they ask for. Create a positive experience that makes people want to come back—and bring others.

Start Now: Take note of how you currently interact with your clients. Are you meeting their needs? Are you reliable and professional? If not, make a conscious effort to improve. Start small—be punctual, stay off your phone during cuts, and communicate clearly with each customer.

TIP 4: BE READY TO SEIZE OPPORTUNITIES

Pay attention to other barbers' clients in your shop. If someone is unhappy with their barber or can't wait, be prepared to step in and deliver a great haircut that will win them over.

Start Now: Start conversations with all clients in the shop— not just your own. Observe what they're getting done, and think about how you'd approach their cut. The next time someone gives you an opening, take it, and show them what you can do.

HOW TO START TAKING ACTION TODAY

The best way to put these tips into practice is by focusing on what you can control *now*. Identify one skill you need to sharpen— maybe it's perfecting your fade or improving your customer service—and start working on it today. Take small, consistent steps: practice cuts, invest in modern tools, and create a game plan for delivering better service. By committing to constant improvement, you'll build a reputation that brings clients through your door and keeps them coming back.

Chapter 4
Charge What You're Worth: Getting Top Dollar!

HOW TO ASSESS AND INCREASE YOUR VALUE AS A BARBER

One of the first things you need to focus on as a barber isn't the money—it's building your skills. While this book is about helping you make $100,000 or more as a barber, it's important to understand that even making $60,000 or $70,000 a year is an excellent accomplishment. But to get there, the first focus should be improving your craft.

As you sharpen your skills, you'll start to build value in your work. With that value comes the ability to pick and choose your clients, but I want to be clear—this doesn't mean discriminating against people who want to pay you for your services. What it does mean is learning how to navigate your business, so it works for you. Remember, you're not running a charity; you're running a business.

START BY BUILDING A CLIENTELE

In the beginning, you have to take everyone who comes into your chair. At this stage, your focus isn't on being selective—it's about getting traffic, building your reputation, and keeping your chair busy.

Once you've built a steady income, you can start narrowing down your clientele to those who fit your goals and align with the value you provide. Here's how it worked for me:

After I built a solid clientele, with everyone calling my name, "Hey, Butter, can I get in your chair?" I started being more selective.

I focused on accepting clients who tipped well or paid higher rates. For example, if someone wanted to be in my chair for an hour and being picky, but only paying $20 or $25, I had to question if that was worth my time. Over time I would not satisfy headache clients intentionally and I began prioritizing clients who valued my services and tipped generously—like those giving $50- $100 for a haircut.

HOW TO LEVERAGE YOUR TIME AND INCREASE EARNINGS

Time management is critical in this business. For me, I aim to finish most haircuts in 15–20 minutes and spend no more than 30 minutes on a haircut with a beard trim. Here's how I break it down:

- I charge a minimum of $30 for a haircut.
- If I'm doing a beard trim, I add $10.
- I expect at least a $10 tip for the service.

That brings me to $50 per client, and I can complete the service in 20–30 minutes.

If a client doesn't tip or doesn't value my time, I don't prioritize them. Over time, this strategy helped me avoid burnout and allowed me to make significant money as a barber.

START HUMBLE, THEN BUILD UP

Some barbers make the mistake of charging $40 or $50 per haircut right out of the gate. Unless you've already built a strong reputation, that's unrealistic. When you're just starting, focus on volume, not price. As your demand increases and your skills improve, you'll naturally be able to raise your rates without losing too many clients.

For example, if you start at $10 per cut and serve 60 clients a week, you're earning $600. Once you've improved your skills and built demand, you can increase your price to $20 per cut. Even if you lose some clients and drop to 40 clients a week, you're still making $800—more than before.

When your schedule starts filling up at $20 per cut, you can increase your price to $30 per cut. Let's say you lose another 10 clients and drop to 30 clients per week—that's $900 per week, and you're working less.

This is the process of building your value and increasing your rates. It's a cycle: raise your prices, adjust to the drop-off, and attract

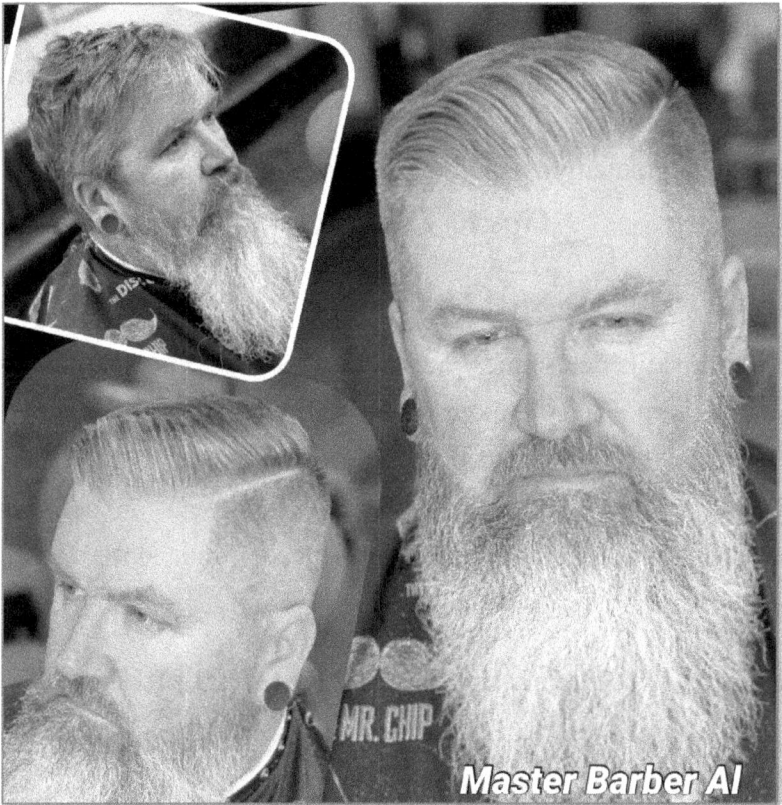

new clients who are willing to pay your rates. Over time, this strategy positions you to earn top dollar while maintaining a manageable workload.

ADAPTING TO YOUR MARKET

Your pricing also depends on the area you're in and the value the community associates with your work. If you're in a new market, you may need to start at a lower price to build a clientele. But as your reputation grows, you can increase your prices to reflect your value.

When I opened a new shop in my 40s, I followed this principle. I started at a competitive rate to attract clients, and within two months, I was doing 20–30 cuts every Friday and Saturday, covering my rent and more. It's all about starting where you are, proving your worth, and gradually raising your rates as your demand increases.

Tips to Take Action Now

TIP 1: FOCUS ON SKILLS FIRST, NOT MONEY

Your skills determine your value. The better you are, the more you can charge, and the more people will seek you out.

Start Now: Dedicate time to improving your craft. Practice different styles, learn new techniques, and focus on delivering consistent quality. Build your confidence in your skills, because that's what drives your value.

TIP 2: BUILD VOLUME BEFORE RAISING PRICES

Start with a lower price to attract clients and build a steady flow of traffic. Then, gradually increase your rates as your demand grows.

Start Now: Evaluate your current pricing and demand. If you're new, focus on filling your chair first. If your chair is consistently full, consider raising your rates slightly and see how your clients respond.

TIP 3: PRIORITIZE CLIENTS WHO VALUE YOU

Not every client is worth your time. Over time, focus on building a clientele that appreciates your work and pays accordingly.

Start Now: Take note of which clients tip well and respect your time. As you grow, prioritize these clients in your schedule and gradually phase out those who don't align with your goals.

TIP 4: MANAGE YOUR TIME EFFECTIVELY

Efficiency is key to maximizing your earnings without burning out. Learn to deliver high-quality cuts in a shorter amount of time. Preferably, less than 30 minutes for each haircut you offer.

Start Now: Time your cuts and aim to improve your speed without sacrificing quality. Set clear expectations with clients about the time you need for their cut and stick to it.

HOW TO START TAKING ACTION TODAY

Understanding your worth as a barber starts with building your skills and reputation. Focus on delivering quality work to every client and managing your time effectively. Begin with a lower price to attract clients, then gradually increase your rates as your demand grows. Prioritize clients who value your work, and don't be afraid to adjust your clientele over time. By following these steps, you'll position yourself to earn more while doing what you love.

Chapter 5
Your Ticket to Wealth:
Building a Loyal Clientele

Now that you understand the kind of clientele you want to focus on, let's dive into how to build that clientele from scratch. A lot of barbers struggle with getting started, and this chapter will focus on practical strategies and examples to help you hit the ground running. Before you can charge premium prices and attract your ideal clients, you need to put yourself out there, build awareness, and earn trust.

One of the biggest mistakes I see with new barbers is sitting in the shop for hours, waiting for clients to magically walk through the door. This approach gets you nowhere. It's even worse when barbers spend that time playing video games, scrolling through social media, or watching movies on their phones. Unless you're using that time to watch educational videos or learning how to market yourself, you're wasting valuable opportunities.

When I opened my third barbershop in 2017 in the Poconos, Pennsylvania—a place where I didn't know a single person—I relied on a strategy I had developed from my first two shops. I didn't sit around waiting for clients to show up. I hit the streets.

HITTING THE STREETS TO BUILD A NAME

I would walk outside my barbershop and introduce myself to people. I'd say something like, "Hi, my name is Master Barber Al. I'm new in the area, and I'm offering free haircuts in exchange for letting me take a picture of the cut to share on social media. This way, I can show others the quality of my work."

Out of every 10 people I talked to, at least two or three would take me up on the offer. This approach worked for a few reasons:

- **It offered value:** Free haircuts are hard to turn down.
- **It built trust:** People liked that I was confident enough to share pictures of my work.
- **It showcased my skills:** I always had previous haircut photos on my phone to show potential clients.

Here's something I will admit. When I first started at my third barbershop in 2017, some of the haircut pictures I showed weren't my own. I reached out to my brother, who runs a barbershop in Virginia, and asked him if I could use photos of cuts from one of his barbers. He agreed, and I downloaded some pictures from their social media. For the first 20 or so clients, I used those photos as my own to show people what I was capable of. No one ever questioned if the cuts were mine or not.

Once I started cutting hair and taking my own photos, I replaced those borrowed pictures with my own work. Within two or three weeks, my phone was filled with photos of my actual cuts, which I began uploading to a new social media account.

GROWING FAST THROUGH EFFORT AND STRATEGY

In less than two months, I had a steady flow of clients. The waiting area in my shop was full, my rent was covered, and by the third month, I was profitable. I'll talk more about how to set up and manage a shop in Phase 2 of this book, but for now, it's important to understand the relentless effort I put into building my clientele.

WHY WALK-INS ARE CRITICAL FOR NEW BARBERS

If you're just starting out, avoid being appointment-only in the beginning. When no one knows who you are, you need to be available for walk-ins. Every person who walks into the shop is a potential new client. If you're locked into appointments, you might miss opportunities to get new people into your chair.

Walk-ins give you a chance to showcase your skills, build relationships, and start creating regular clients. As you grow, you can shift to appointments, but in the early stages, flexibility is key.

THE POWER OF FLYERS

I know it might seem old school, but flyers are still effective. Not everyone is on social media, and a physical flyer gives you a tangible way to make an impression. I recommend creating 5,000 flyers for under $150.

On these flyers, include your best haircut photos, your location, your social media, and your contact information. When I was out in public, I'd hand these flyers to people I met. Flyers are more effective than business cards because they're bigger and allow you to showcase your work. Business cards are great for existing clients, but when meeting someone for the first time, a flyer with pictures of your cuts has more impact.

OFFERING INCENTIVES TO NEW CLIENTS

Another way to attract clients is by offering special deals. Here are a few examples:

- Offer the first haircut at half price.
- Tell clients they can bring a friend, and one of them gets their haircut for free.
- Offer a free haircut after they come to you twice.

These types of promotions give people a reason to choose you over someone else, especially if they've never been in your chair before.

MAKING CONNECTIONS EVERYWHERE YOU GO

When I was opening my shop in the Poconos, I talked to people everywhere—at Walmart, the gas station, the grocery store. People would come into the shop and say, "Hey Al, you gave me a flyer at Walmart!" or "You stopped me on Main Street and told me you cut hair."

To be honest, I didn't always remember everyone I talked to because I was speaking to so many people every day. But what mattered was that they remembered me, and it brought them through my doors.

CONSISTENCY LEADS TO SUCCESS

Within a few short months, I had built a steady clientele in a place where I started with zero connections. I achieved this by being relentless, going out into the community, and making personal connections. This approach not only filled my chair but also built a reputation that kept clients coming back.

Tips to Take Action Now

TIP 1: GET OUT OF THE SHOP AND INTO THE COMMUNITY

Don't waste hours sitting in the shop waiting for clients. Go out and introduce yourself to people in the area. Offer free or discounted cuts to get people into your chair.

Start Now: Make it a goal to talk to at least 10 new people every day. Introduce yourself, hand out flyers, and showcase your work.

TIP 2: USE FLYERS TO SHOWCASE YOUR WORK

Flyers are an affordable and effective way to market yourself, especially to people who aren't on social media.

Start Now: Design a flyer with your best haircut photos, location, social media and contact information. Order 5,000 flyers (4x6 Size Recommended, Full Color, 2 sided) and start handing them out in high-traffic areas.

Master Barber Al

TIP 3: OFFER INCENTIVES TO NEW CLIENTS

People love a good deal, especially when trying something new. Offer promotions to make it easier for potential clients to choose you.

Start Now: Create a simple promotion, like half-price cuts for first-time clients or "bring a friend" deals. Advertise these incentives on your flyers and social media.

TIP 4: BE FLEXIBLE AND TAKE WALK-INS

Appointments are great once you're established, but in the beginning, walk-ins are essential for building a steady flow of clients.

Start Now: Make yourself available for walk-ins. Focus on creating a great experience for every person who sits in your chair so they want to come back.

HOW TO START TAKING ACTION TODAY

Building a clientele takes effort, strategy, and consistency. Get out into the community, hand out flyers, and talk to as many people as possible. Use social media to showcase your work and offer promotions to attract new clients. By putting in the effort now, you'll create a foundation for long-term success in the barbering business.

Chapter 6
7 Proven Ways to Pack Your Chair with Customers

In this chapter, I'll share seven proven strategies to grow your clientele and keep your chair full. These strategies are practical and effective, whether you're trying to bring in new clients or get walk-ins to choose your chair. Each of these has been personally tested by me and other barbers, and they all work. *(Note: Some can be seen as unethical, so use at your discretion, Lol)*

1. THE WALK-IN GREETER

Every new face that walks into your shop should be greeted warmly. Many barbers miss this opportunity, sitting silently and waiting for the customer to make the first move. That's a mistake. Instead, as soon as someone walks in, say:

"Hey, how you doing? My name is [Your Name], and I'm one of the barbers here. Are you looking for a haircut today?"

This simple introduction breaks the ice and makes the person feel welcome. Even if they don't choose your chair immediately, they'll remember the friendly interaction.

If they're undecided, encourage them to take a moment: "No problem if you're just looking around. Feel free to sit and relax. Let me know if you have any questions."

Why It Works:
- Builds rapport instantly.
- Creates trust and makes clients more likely to choose you over others.

Story Example:

I've seen shops where walk-ins get ignored, or worse, stared at awkwardly. That's not how you want to operate. By being proactive and approachable, I've converted countless walk-ins into loyal clients.

2. THE OBSERVER

This strategy involves observing other barbers while they're cutting hair. It's subtle but effective. When clients notice you watching their haircut, it shows you're paying attention to their preferences. If their regular barber isn't available, you become the next logical choice.

How It Works:

- Position yourself where the client can see you watching.
- Avoid being intrusive or making the other barber uncomfortable.
- If their regular barber steps away, let the client decide whether to wait or sit in your chair.

Why It Works:

- Builds trust without being aggressive.
- Positions you as a backup option when their regular barber isn't available.

Story Example:

In my early days, I used this strategy often. I'd notice a client whose barber wasn't available on Sundays or during lunch breaks. Because they'd seen me observing their cuts, they'd naturally come to me. Many of them became long-term clients.

3. SHARK MODE

Shark mode is all about hustle and going after clients proactively. It's especially useful in competitive shops where you need to stand out.

How It Works:

- Stand outside the shop and greet people walking by.
- Say something like, "Hey, getting a cut today?" before they even reach the shop.
- Create opportunities to bring clients in before other barbers get the chance.

Why It Works:

- Shows initiative and builds rapport before the client even enters the shop.
- Effective in busy areas with high foot traffic.

Story Example:

My friend Sam was the master of Shark Mode. He'd start conversations with people several storefronts away, creating a connection before they even walked into the shop. While other barbers frowned on it, Sam's chair was always full because of his proactive approach.

4. THE NAME CALL

The name call is a clever strategy to create familiarity and keep other barbers from approaching potential clients.

How It Works:

- When you see someone walking in, say, "Hey, what's up, Jack?" even if you don't know their name.

- If they respond and sit in your chair, casually say, "Oh, I thought you were someone else. What's your name?"

Why It Works:
- Creates an instant connection.
- Deters other barbers from competing for the client, thinking you know them personally.

Story Example:

I learned this trick from Sam. For months, I thought he knew everyone who walked in, but one day I realized it was a tactic. By calling out random names, he made people feel welcomed and created an illusion of familiarity.

5. SOCIAL PROOF

Perception is everything. Clients are drawn to barbers who look professional and prepared. From your appearance to your workstation, everything should convey confidence and competence.

What to Do:
- Wear a barber jacket and keep your tools organized.
- Display quality products and equipment at your station, even if you don't use them all.
- Maintain a clean and professional appearance.

Why It Works:
- Instantly builds trust with new clients.
- Helps you stand out in a competitive environment.

Story Example:

When I hired Fred, an older barber, in my first shop, I noticed older clients gravitated toward him. Fred wore a barber jacket, kept his station immaculate, and even had a lather machine. Although his fades weren't as sharp as mine, his professionalism attracted a loyal clientele.

6. THE STALL

When business is slow, use your time wisely to create the illusion of busyness. Slow down your pace and add extra touches to the haircut, making it appear that the shop is active.

How It Works:

- Take your time with clients when there's foot traffic outside the shop.
- Add small details like styling or refining edges to make the service stand out.

Why It Works:

- Makes the shop appear busy and in demand.
- Encourages passersby to come in, thinking it's a popular spot.

Story Example:

In my first shop, we had a large window facing the street. Whenever people stopped to look inside, I'd slow down my cuts and make the process look detailed. Many times, those onlookers would come in later that week and become clients.

7. FLYERS WITH YOUR IMAGE

Flyers may seem old-fashioned, but they're highly effective for marketing your services. Including your photo on the flyer makes it personal and ensures clients know exactly who to ask for when they walk in.

How It Works:

- Create a 4x6 flyer with your photo, contact information, and pictures of your work.
- Add an incentive like "50% off for first-time clients."
- Distribute flyers in high-traffic areas like malls, grocery stores, and restaurants.

Why It Works:

- Increases visibility and builds your personal brand.
- Encourages walk-ins to ask for you specifically.

Story Example:

When I was starting out, I handed out flyers everywhere—at Walmart, local restaurants, and busy streets. People often came into the shop saying, "I'm looking for this guy," pointing to my picture on the flyer.

Tips to Take Action Now

TIP 1: GREET EVERY WALK-IN

A warm introduction goes a long way. Make it a habit to greet every walk-in personally and build rapport.

Start Now: Next time someone walks in, introduce yourself with confidence and offer your services.

TIP 2: LOOK PROFESSIONAL

Your appearance and workstation reflect your skills. Invest in a barber jacket and keep your tools clean and organized.

Start Now: Clean up your station, organize your tools, and consider upgrading your wardrobe to look more professional.

TIP 3: DISTRIBUTE FLYERS

Flyers with your photo and work examples can help you stand out. Include a special offer to attract first-time clients.

Start Now: Design a flyer with your photo, contact info, and best cuts. Start distributing them in high-traffic areas.

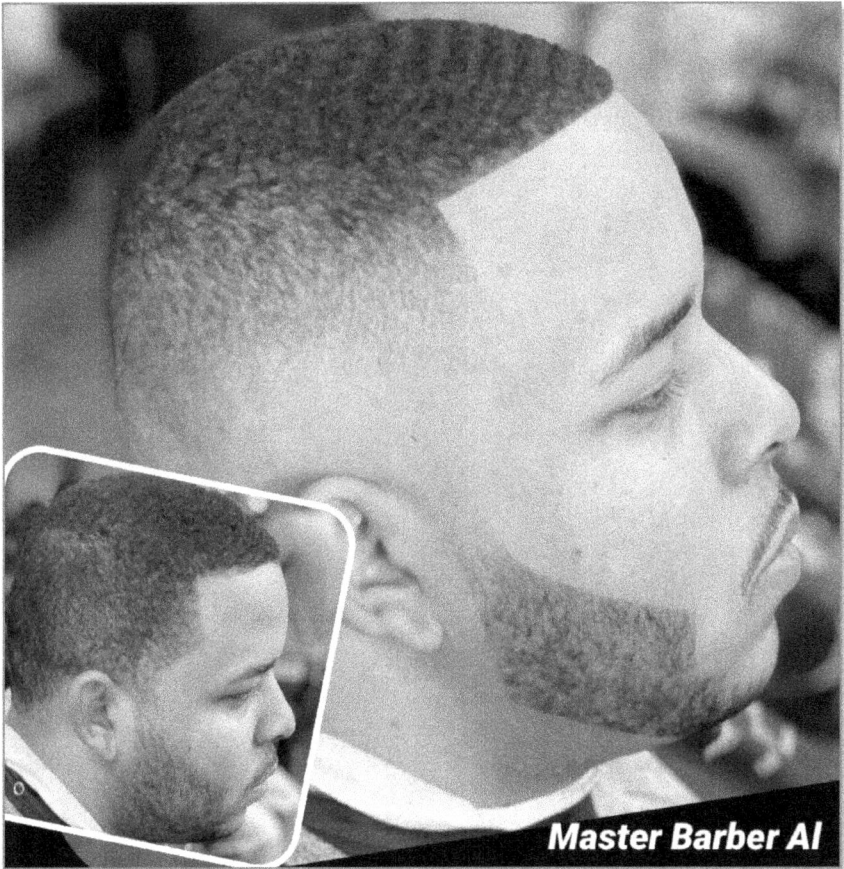

Master Barber Al

TIP 4: BE PROACTIVE

Use strategies like Shark Mode and the Name Call to engage potential clients and bring them into your chair.

Start Now: Step outside your shop and start conversations with people nearby. Practice greeting them confidently.

HOW TO START IMPLEMENTING THESE STRATEGIES

Consistency is the key to success. Start by focusing on one or two strategies, like greeting walk-ins or distributing flyers, and build from there. These strategies work best when combined, so over time, incorporate all seven into your routine. Within months, you'll notice a significant difference in your clientele and income.

Chapter 7
The Must-Have Barber Skills
That Keep Clients Coming Back

At this point in the book, I hope you're getting valuable insights to grow your clientele and enhance your skills as a barber. The strategies I've shared so far have worked for me and will work for you if you put them into practice. In this chapter, I'll dive into four critical skills every barber should master to create strong client relationships, build trust, and keep your chair full.

These aren't just about cutting hair—they're personal skills that go beyond the technical aspects of barbering. The four skills are:

1. The Ability to Listen
2. The Ability to Communicate and Speak
3. The Art of Mimicking
4. Time Management

Each of these skills plays a unique role in connecting with your clients and growing your business. Let's break them down in detail.

1. THE ABILITY TO LISTEN

Listening is a skill that's often underestimated but incredibly important in barbering. Many barbers focus solely on the haircut, missing opportunities to connect with their clients on a deeper level. Listening goes beyond understanding how your client wants their hair done—it's about hearing them as a person.

Why It Matters:

- Builds rapport and breaks down barriers, especially with new clients.

- Gives clients an outlet to share their stories, frustrations, or triumphs, creating a memorable experience.
- Helps clients feel valued, which increases loyalty and tips.

Example:

I've had countless clients open up about their lives in my chair. Whether it's about their spouse, kids, job, or community, they share personal stories because I make them feel heard. Even if you give them the sharpest haircut of their life, if they feel dismissed or ignored, they might not come back.

PRACTICAL TIP:

Pay attention to their tone and body language. Are they looking to vent, or are they the quiet type? Adapt your listening style to their needs.

2. THE ABILITY TO COMMUNICATE AND SPEAK

Communication goes hand in hand with listening. It's not about being a psychologist or having a degree—it's about showing that you care. When clients share their thoughts, respond in a way that makes them feel understood and appreciated.

Why It Matters:
- Helps build trust and a stronger connection with clients.
- Turns a haircut into a full experience, making clients more likely to return.
- Opens the door for referrals because clients will recommend you as someone who not only provides great cuts but also great conversations.

Example:

If a client shares a tough situation they're going through, like problems at work, your response doesn't need to be groundbreaking. A simple, "Man, that sounds rough. I hope things get better," can make a huge difference. It shows you're paying attention and that you care.

Practical Tip:

Practice active listening. Nod, make eye contact, and ask follow-up questions. Even a small comment like "Tell me more about that" shows you're engaged.

3. THE ART OF MIMICKING

Mimicking is a subtle but powerful skill. It's about matching your client's energy, tone, and body language to create a subconscious connection. People naturally gravitate toward others who reflect their own behavior and energy, even if they don't realize it.

Why It Matters:

- Builds a subconscious bond that makes clients feel comfortable.
- Enhances your ability to relate to clients, making them more likely to trust you.
- Increases loyalty because clients feel like you "get" them.

How to Mimic:

- Match their tone: If they're upbeat and energetic, mirror that energy. If they're calm and reserved, dial it down.

- Match their body language: If they lean forward while talking, do the same. If they gesture with their hands, mirror that subtly.

Example:

A client comes in and says, "Man, I've had a rough day." Match their tone and respond with, "Yeah, I feel you—it's been one of those days for me too." This creates an instant connection because you've aligned yourself with their experience.

Advanced Tip:

When a client shares a story, respond with a relatable one of your own. For example, if they talk about their teenager acting out, share a story about your niece or nephew. This makes them feel understood and deepens the connection.

4. TIME MANAGEMENT

Time management is one of the most overlooked skills in barbering. Being on time and efficient with your work shows respect for your clients' time and builds your reputation as a professional.

Why It Matters:

- Keeps your schedule running smoothly and prevents long wait times.
- Builds trust with clients, knowing they can rely on you to stick to your hours.
- Attracts more clients because they know you value their time.

Key Time Management Habits:

- **Consistent Hours:** Always open and close your shop at the scheduled times. If you advertise 9 AM to 9 PM, stick to it—even on slow days.
- **Be Punctual:** Never leave clients waiting. If you're running late, communicate with them.
- **Move Lines Quickly:** When you have a busy schedule, focus on efficiency without sacrificing quality.

Example:

When I was starting out, my shop manager fined barbers for being late because clients were left waiting. I never received a fine—except for one time when I caught a ride with Sam, who made us late. That experience taught me the importance of being responsible for my own time.

What to Avoid:

- Leaving clients unattended mid-haircut. Taking a long phone call while a client is in the chair is unprofessional and disrespectful.
- Being inconsistent with your hours. If clients don't know when you're available, they'll look for someone else.

Tips to Take Action Now

TIP 1: LISTEN ACTIVELY TO YOUR CLIENTS

Listening is more than just hearing—it's about engaging with your clients and showing genuine interest in what they're saying.

Start Now: The next time a client talks about their day, ask follow-up questions or share a similar story to show you're paying attention.

TIP 2: COMMUNICATE WITH CARE

Effective communication makes your clients feel valued and understood.

Start Now: Practice responding to client stories with empathy and positivity. For example, if they share a challenge, respond with encouragement or understanding.

TIP 3: MIMIC AND RELATE

Matching your clients' tone and energy creates a subconscious connection that builds trust.

Start Now: Observe your next client's energy level and tone. Mirror it subtly in your responses and body language.

TIP 4: MASTER TIME MANAGEMENT

Respect your clients' time by being punctual and efficient.

Start Now: Review your daily schedule and identify ways to streamline your workflow. Commit to opening and closing your shop at the advertised times.

CONCLUSION: SKILLS THAT BUILD CONNECTIONS

Mastering these four skills—listening, communicating, mimicking, and time management—will set you apart as a barber. These are the foundations of building rapport and creating a loyal client base. By implementing these skills consistently, you'll not only grow your clientele but also create lasting relationships that keep people coming back.

Chapter 8
Customer Service Hacks
to Boost Your Earnings

Customer service is the foundation of any successful business, and for barbers, it's the key to building lasting relationships and boosting profits. This chapter dives into the strategies I've used to create an exceptional customer experience that not only retains clients but also turns them into your greatest promoters.

MAKE CUSTOMERS FEEL AT HOME

The moment a customer walks into your shop, they should feel welcomed and comfortable. This isn't just about good manners; it's about setting the tone for their entire experience. Whether it's a new face or a loyal regular, the approach should be the same.

When a customer enters, someone should immediately acknowledge them. Even if you're busy, a quick "Hey, how's it going? Someone will be right with you" goes a long way. If they're a returning customer, a personalized greeting like, "Good to see you again! How's everything?" makes them feel valued.

If the shop is crowded and there's a wait, let them know you've noticed them and offer something to make the wait more enjoyable. For example:

- Encourage them to change the TV channel or put on a movie.
- Direct them to magazines or other available amenities.
- If you have snacks, coffee, or other small comforts, let them know they're welcome to help themselves.

These small gestures show that you care about their experience from the moment they walk in, even if they're not in the chair yet.

THE POWER OF FEEDBACK

As business owners, we can sometimes assume we know what's best for our customers, but feedback often reveals things we miss. Customers come with a wealth of experience from visiting other barbershops, and their insights can be invaluable.

One simple way to gather feedback is through cards or forms where customers can rate their experience or suggest improvements. Here's an example: You might ask, "What's one thing we could improve?" or "Is there anything that would make your visit more enjoyable?" One customer might suggest that the music is always too loud, and the barbers do not greet you when they walk in. This may seem to make the shop not that inviting and not feel too friendly.

Feedback doesn't just improve your shop; it builds trust. When customers see you're genuinely interested in their opinions, they're more likely to feel loyal to your business.

OFFER EXTRA TREATMENT

Going above and beyond for your customers adds significant value to their experience. People remember the small details that make them feel special. For instance:

- Offer complimentary grooming products like hair gel or cream after a cut.
- Have a selection of colognes available for customers who want a quick spritz before leaving.
- Include services like a warm towel treatment or a brief scalp massage for free.

These extras don't have to cost you much, but they create a perception of luxury and care. When customers feel like they're getting more value than they paid for, they're far more likely to return—and to spread the word.

LEVERAGE REFERRALS WITH INCENTIVES

Word of mouth is one of the most powerful tools for growing your business, and referral programs can amplify it. Offer incentives to encourage your current customers to bring in new clients. For example:

- "Bring a friend and get half off your next haircut."
- "Come in five times, and your sixth cut is free."

These promotions not only attract new clients but also keep your existing ones coming back. It's a win-win that helps you build momentum, especially during slower periods.

COLLECT CONTACT INFORMATION

In today's world, staying connected with your customers is easier—and more important—than ever. Emails and text messages are invaluable tools for promoting your shop, sharing special offers, and maintaining relationships.

Here's how to gather contact information:

1. **Feedback Cards**: Ask for their email or phone number in exchange for a small gift, like a discount on their next visit.
2. **Sign-Up Incentives**: Offer a free product or service for joining your mailing list.

Once you have their contact information, use it wisely:

- Send out email or text blasts about slow-day specials, such as "20% off on Tuesdays."
- Announce new services or products you're offering.
- Share updates about the shop, like extended hours or upcoming events.

A solid contact list not only drives more traffic to your shop but also opens the door for future business opportunities. For example, if you develop a product like a bump cream or hair tonic, you already have a ready-made audience to market it to.

EXPAND BEYOND HAIRCUTS

While your primary business is cutting hair, don't limit yourself to just that. Think about other ways to serve your clients and increase revenue. For instance:

- Develop a line of grooming products, like beard oils or shampoos.
- Offer gift cards or membership packages that include multiple services.

The more value you provide, the more likely customers are to see your shop as their go-to destination for all their grooming needs.

THE ROAD TO SKYROCKETING YOUR PROFITS

Great customer service isn't just about keeping your current clients happy; it's about turning every interaction into an opportunity to grow your business. From making customers feel at home to leveraging feedback, offering extras, and building a solid contact list, these strategies lay the foundation for long-term success.

The key is consistency. When you create an experience that's memorable and exceeds expectations, customers won't just come back—they'll bring others with them. With these tools in your arsenal, you're well on your way to boosting both your profits and your reputation.

Tips to Take Action Now

TIP 1: CREATE A COMFORTABLE ENVIRONMENT

Greet every client warmly and ensure your shop feels inviting.

Start Now: Assess your shop's layout and atmosphere. Add small touches like coffee, magazines, or a simple TV remote to make clients feel at home.

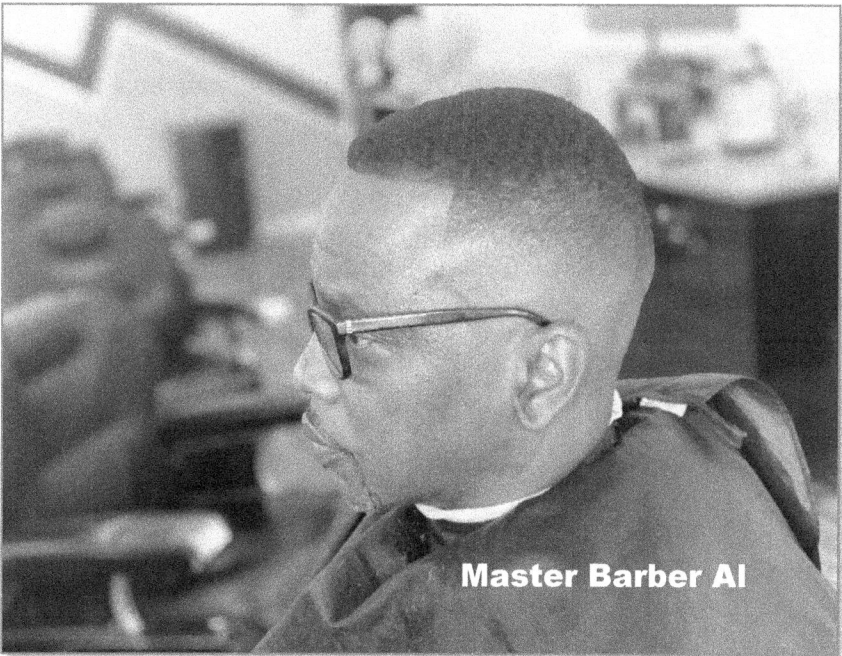

Master Barber Al

TIP 2: COLLECT FEEDBACK AND CONTACT INFORMATION

Ask your clients what they think and use their insights to improve.

Start Now: Design a feedback card or set up an online feedback form. Offer a small incentive for their participation, like a discount or a free service.

TIP 3: ADD VALUE WITH EXTRA TREATMENTS

Surprise your clients with complimentary services or products.

Start Now: Choose one small extra to include with your next few haircuts, like a quick cologne spritz or a hot towel treatment.

TIP 4: LEVERAGE REFERRALS

Encourage your existing clients to bring in new ones with incentives.

Start Now: Create a simple referral program and let your clients know about it. Start with something easy, like "Bring a friend, and you both get $5 off."

Tip 5: Build and Use Your Contact List

Stay in touch with your clients through regular emails or text promotions.

Start Now: Begin collecting contact info from your clients today. Send out your first email promotion within the next two weeks.

CONCLUSION: CUSTOMER SERVICE IS KEY TO PROFITABILITY

Exceptional customer service goes beyond the basics. It's about making every client feel valued, comfortable, and eager to return. By implementing these strategies, you can transform your barbershop into a space that not only attracts new clients but also keeps them coming back for more.

Chapter 9
How Barbershop Culture Drives Profits

The environment and culture of your barbershop play a critical role in attracting and retaining customers. A well-maintained, welcoming space can foster client loyalty, while a chaotic or unprofessional atmosphere can drive potential customers away. In this chapter, we'll explore what kind of culture and environment are most conducive to growth and profitability.

FIRST IMPRESSIONS MATTER

When a customer walks into your shop, the first impression they get often determines whether they'll stay or leave.

Example:

I recently visited a barbershop to inquire about chair rental prices. The moment I stepped in, the music was blaring, and I couldn't hear myself think. Despite making eye contact with someone who appeared to be the manager, nothing was done to turn down the volume. I had to walk up to the front and almost yell to ask my question. It was unprofessional and made me realize I'd never want to work or get my haircut there.

Key Takeaway:

Create a peaceful, welcoming environment. Peacefulness never offends, whereas chaos—like loud music or unruly behavior—can alienate clients.

SET THE TONE WITH NO PROFANITY POLICIES

A professional atmosphere requires a certain level of decorum. Profanity can drive away customers who value a respectful and family-friendly environment.

Example:

In one of my shops, I hung large "No Profanity" signs that were visible from the window. I had clients tell me they decided to visit because they saw the signs and appreciated the policy. Parents especially felt comfortable bringing their kids in, knowing they wouldn't be exposed to inappropriate language.

One time, a guy walked in and immediately cursed while asking about prices. I politely pointed to the no-profanity sign. He paused, then cursed again. He looked around with a confused expression, as if thinking, "I don't know how to speak without cursing," and then walked out. While it was amusing to witness his limited vocabulary, it reinforced the importance of setting boundaries for the shop's culture.

Key Takeaway:

A profanity-free zone creates a respectful atmosphere that appeals to a wider range of clients, including families and professionals.

FOSTER A POSITIVE ATMOSPHERE

Your shop's atmosphere should feel inviting and safe for everyone, regardless of age, gender, or background.

- **Keep Conversations Neutral:**
  Stick to non-controversial topics like sports, entertainment, or current events. Avoid divisive

subjects like religion and politics, which can lead to arguments or conflicts.

- **Be Mindful of Music:**
- While hip-hop might appeal to some clients, it could alienate others. Balance your playlist with softer music, news channels, or neutral radio stations to create a space that welcomes everyone.

Example:

In one of my shops, I played Lite FM and kept the atmosphere neutral. This approach attracted clients from all backgrounds—Hispanic, Indian, African American, and others. The diversity was a testament to the inclusive environment I cultivated. Even clients who loved hip-hop still came because they valued the quality of the cuts.

Key Takeaway:

Create a balanced environment where everyone feels comfortable, regardless of their personal preferences.

MAINTAIN PROFESSIONAL STAFF BEHAVIOR

The behavior of your staff has a significant impact on your shop's culture. Inappropriate or offensive actions can tarnish your shop's reputation.

Example:

When I was younger, my coworkers and I would talk in coded language about women who entered the shop. While we thought it was harmless because we were talking about car parts, I later realized how inappropriate it was and how easily someone could pick up on it. As I matured, I set stricter standards for behavior in my shops.

Key Takeaway:

Ensure all barbers understand the importance of professionalism. Inappropriate conversations or behavior should never be tolerated.

NEUTRAL DÉCOR AND AMBIANCE

The physical look and feel of your shop contribute to its overall culture.

- **Color Scheme:**
  Use bright, neutral colors like white or off-white to create a friendly, clean environment. Avoid dark or overly bold colors that might make the space feel uninviting.

- **Décor:**
  Keep your shop organized and clutter-free. A clean, professional appearance builds trust with clients.

Example:

One client feedback card mentioned they avoided a particular barbershop because the dark red walls made the space feel oppressive. Simple adjustments to décor can make a big difference in how clients perceive your space.

Key Takeaway:

Invest in a clean, neutral, and inviting physical space to enhance the customer experience.

Tips to Take Action Now

TIP 1: PRIORITIZE FIRST IMPRESSIONS

Ensure every client is greeted warmly and made to feel welcome.

Start Now: Walk through your shop as if you're a new customer. Identify anything that might feel uninviting, like loud music or clutter, and address it immediately.

TIP 2: ENFORCE A NO PROFANITY POLICY

A respectful atmosphere encourages families and professionals to visit your shop.

Start Now: Create visible "No Profanity" signs and discuss the policy with your staff. Lead by example and correct inappropriate behavior when necessary.

TIP 3: KEEP TOPICS NEUTRAL AND ENGAGING

Avoid controversial discussions that could alienate clients.

Start Now: Encourage your barbers to engage clients in light, neutral conversations about sports, entertainment, or current events.

TIP 4: BALANCE YOUR MUSIC CHOICES

Cater to a diverse clientele by playing music or content that appeals to a broad audience.

Start Now: Evaluate your current playlist or TV programming. Incorporate softer music or neutral channels like news or sports.

TIP 5: MAINTAIN CLEANLINESS AND NEUTRAL DÉCOR

A clean, well-lit space fosters trust and professionalism.

Start Now: Take a fresh look at your shop's décor and cleanliness. Consider repainting walls in brighter colors and decluttering workspaces to create a more inviting environment.

CONCLUSION: A CULTURE THAT ATTRACTS AND RETAINS CLIENTS

The culture and environment of your barbershop are just as important as the quality of your cuts. A welcoming, professional space can draw in clients from all walks of life and keep them coming back. By prioritizing respect, cleanliness, and inclusivity, you'll create a shop culture that not only grows your business but also enhances your reputation.

Chapter 10
What Gets You More Cash:
Booth Rent vs. Commission

Every barber, whether new to the industry or with years of experience, will eventually have to make a decision about booth rent versus commission. These two structures define how barbers and shop owners work together and, ultimately, how money is made in this business. This chapter is all about breaking down these two payment models, sharing what I've learned from running my shops, and helping you decide which path is best for you.

UNDERSTANDING BOOTH RENT

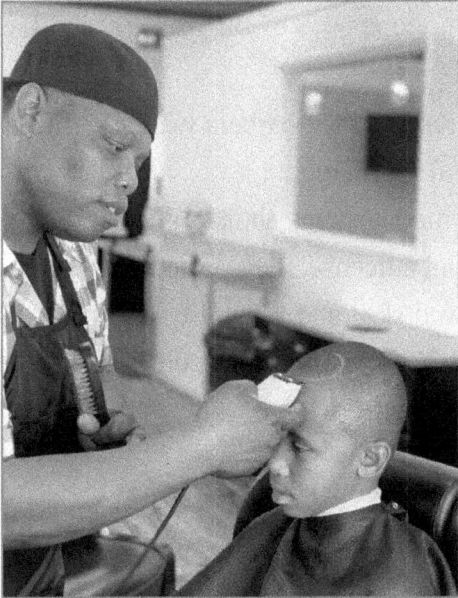

Booth rent is exactly what it sounds like—you rent a chair in a barbershop for a flat weekly or monthly fee. Once you pay that rent, whatever you make from your clients is yours to keep. It's a simple, straightforward agreement.

When I first started researching booth rent, I saw how the rates varied depending on the area. For example, my brother runs a shop in Virginia, and he charges between **$150 and $175 per week** for his barbers. But in my area, I've seen rents climb to **$250 or more per week.** That's why it's so important to know your local market and the volume of traffic the shop can generate.

For barbers who are confident in their ability to bring in steady clients, booth rent can be a great option. You know your costs upfront, and the more you cut, the more you take home. But for beginners who don't have a solid clientele, it can feel like a heavy financial burden.

WHAT IS COMMISSION?

Commission works differently. With commission, you split the income from each haircut with the shop owner. This structure allows you to pay as you earn—if you don't cut hair, you don't owe anything. Commission splits vary, with the most common being:

- **50/50** – A straight split of every haircut.
- **60/40** – The barber keeps 60% of the income, and the shop keeps 40%.
- **70/30** – Typically reserved for barbers with significant experience or a loyal following.

I've implemented all these models in my shops. When I brought on apprentices or barbers without a license, they started with **50/50**. Experienced barbers who showed skill and reliability were moved to **60/40**, and I've even done **70/30** for barbers who consistently met certain quotas.

MY EXPERIENCE AS A SHOP OWNER

Running my own shops gave me a lot of insight into which model works better for a shop owner. Let me share an example from my second shop, which was in a prime location with heavy foot traffic. That shop had four chairs and averaged between **400 and 700 cuts a week**.

On average, I earned **$5 per cut** from commissions. With numbers like that, the math speaks for itself. At 400 cuts, I'd bring in **$2,000 per week.** At 700 cuts, it was **$3,500 per week.** Compare that to booth rent—if I had charged **$200 per week per chair,** I'd only be making **$800 weekly.**

For me, commissions were a no-brainer in a shop like this. It wasn't just about the money—it was about the steady flow of clients and the fact that barbers could easily build their own clientele within my shop. My location did the heavy lifting, bringing in traffic and providing a platform for barbers to thrive.

WHEN BOOTH RENT MAKES SENSE FOR SHOP OWNERS

Not every shop is located on a busy corner with endless walk-ins. If your shop is in a quieter area or has inconsistent traffic, booth rent might be the better option. You'll still make a steady income, regardless of how many clients each barber serves.

For example, if your shop only averages **700 to 900 cuts a month** and you're struggling to fill the chairs, charging **$200 per week for booth rent** might provide more stability than relying on commissions.

WHAT ABOUT BARBERS? WHICH MODEL SHOULD YOU CHOOSE?

For barbers, the decision comes down to your level of experience and the clientele you've built.

When I first started, commission was the way to go. I didn't have a loyal client base, so being in a busy shop gave me the opportunity to prove myself. I could focus on cutting hair and building relationships while the shop took care of the overhead. Over time, as I developed a steady stream of repeat clients, I transitioned to booth rent because it allowed me to keep more of what I earned.

If you're just starting out and don't have a following, commission is a smart choice. Find a shop with plenty of walk-in traffic and a fair split, like **60/40.** This lets you focus on perfecting your craft and growing your reputation.

Once you've built a solid clientele and know how to consistently hit your numbers, booth rent becomes more appealing. Paying **$150 or $200 per week** might seem like a lot at first, but if you're cutting **70 clients a week at $15 per cut,** you'll make **$1,050 weekly**—a huge profit after covering your rent.

STRATEGIES FOR GROWTH

Whether you're working on commission or paying booth rent, the ultimate goal is growth. As a barber, this means growing your clientele, your skills, and eventually your income. As a shop owner, it's about creating an environment where barbers can thrive, which, in turn, boosts your bottom line.

Let me share a quick story about one of my busiest weeks. I remember a time at my second shop when we hit **700 cuts in a single week.** It was a chaotic but exciting experience. Every barber was working non-stop, the waiting area was packed, and the energy in the shop was electric. That kind of traffic is only possible when you invest in your shop's reputation, location, and marketing. For me, it reaffirmed the power of commission in a high-traffic shop.

FINAL THOUGHTS

There's no one-size-fits-all answer when it comes to booth rent versus commission. It's all about knowing your numbers, understanding your market, and making decisions based on your specific goals. As a barber, start with commission to build your base, then transition to booth rent when the time is right. As a shop owner, consider the flow of traffic in your shop and choose the model that maximizes your income while supporting your team.

With the right approach, both barbers and shop owners can find success in either model. It's all about knowing your worth, doing the math, and playing the long game.

Tips to Take Action Now

TIP 1: ASSESS YOUR CURRENT POSITION

Whether you're a barber or a shop owner, understanding where you stand is the first step in deciding between booth rent and commission. Your career stage, client base, and financial goals should all factor into this decision.

Start Now: Evaluate your current clientele. If you're just starting out and don't have a steady stream of clients, look for a commission-based shop with high walk-in traffic. If you have a loyal client base, calculate if booth rent would allow you to earn more while keeping expenses in check.

TIP 2: TRACK YOUR NUMBERS

Knowing your weekly cuts, income, and expenses is critical for making informed decisions. Barbers should calculate how many cuts they need to cover booth rent and turn a profit, while shop owners should track traffic to determine which model maximizes revenue.

Start Now: Keep a detailed log of every haircut you do and how much you earn from each one. Shop owners should track how many clients each barber serves and the shop's overall weekly income. Use this data to adjust your strategy as needed.

TIP 3: BUILD YOUR CLIENTELE

If you're working on commission, focus on building a loyal client base that will follow you wherever you go. This gives you the freedom to transition to booth rent—or even open your own shop—when the time is right.

Start Now: Deliver exceptional service and consistently sharp cuts to every client. Hand out flyers, maintain a strong social media presence, and ask satisfied clients to refer their friends. The more loyal clients you have, the more options you'll have in your career.

TIP 4: CHOOSE THE RIGHT SHOP

The location and culture of your shop can make a big difference in your success. For shop owners, creating a welcoming, professional environment can attract top barbers and more clients.

Start Now: Look for shops with steady walk-in traffic and a good reputation. Shop owners, assess your shop's environment. Is it attracting the right barbers and clients? If not, make changes to improve its appeal and visibility.

TIP 5: PLAN FOR GROWTH

Your career or business doesn't stop with one decision. Whether you're renting a booth, working on commission, or running a shop, always plan for the next stage of growth.

Start Now: Set a goal for how many clients you want to serve each week and work toward building a following. Shop owners, strategize how to increase traffic through marketing, partnerships, or promotions. Growth requires consistent effort, so make it part of your daily routine.

Chapter 11
Location, Location, Cash Flow
Picking the Right Spot

The location of your Barber shop can make or break your business. A strategic location can dramatically increase your income by attracting a steady flow of clients. In this chapter, we'll explore the **10-point checklist** for choosing the perfect location, drawing from personal experiences and insights.

KEY FACTORS FOR CHOOSING THE RIGHT LOCATION

1. **Proximity to Public Transit**
   Buses: Look for locations near major bus routes with multiple lines passing by. More routes mean more visibility and accessibility for potential clients.
   Example: My second shop was near six bus lines, creating a constant flow of potential customers.
   Trains: Having a subway or train station nearby is a game-changer. My shop was right by the F train, bringing in commuters directly from Manhattan.

2. **Nearby Foot Traffic Hotspots**
   Malls, shopping centers, and high-traffic streets are ideal. Being close to popular destinations ensures high visibility.
   Example: My shop was just blocks away from Jamaica Avenue, a bustling shopping hub, and had consistent foot traffic from nearby restaurants and stores.

3. **High Foot Traffic Areas**

   Observe the level of foot traffic before signing a lease.

   Example: When scouting my second location, I noticed the area was cluttered with trash—an unusual sign, but it indicated heavy foot traffic. That translated into lots of potential customers walking by daily.

4. **Restaurants and Stores Nearby**

   Restaurants, grocery stores, and shopping centers draw people to the area.

   Example: My shop was near McDonald's, West Indian restaurants, and Spanish eateries, making it a go-to spot for anyone in the vicinity.

5. **Stoplights and Intersections**

   Locations near stoplights or busy intersections are goldmines for visibility. Cars stopped at red lights give drivers time to notice your shop.

   Example: Many clients said they found my shop after noticing it while waiting at a stoplight.

6. **Proximity to Schools**

   High schools, colleges, and even elementary schools bring in steady business.

   Example: My shop was near Hillcrest High School and other schools. Running student specials filled the shop on slower days like Tuesdays and Wednesdays.

7. **City Locations vs. Small Towns**

   Cities provide a larger customer base with more diversity and spending power. Small towns may have fewer clients and repeat customers but can still work if they have key attractions or limited competition.

Example: Queens had no shortage of people willing to travel for a good Barber, even if it meant using public transit.

8. **Shop Visibility**

Avoid locations tucked away on side streets. Aim for high-traffic, easily visible areas, even if they come with a slightly higher rent.

Example: I would always opt for paying $300-$400 more for a prime location. That visibility could generate an extra $500 or more per week in revenue.

HOW TO EVALUATE A LOCATION

Spend time observing the area's foot traffic, especially during peak hours.

Check for nearby amenities like malls, schools, and restaurants.

Ask potential customers where they currently get their haircuts and why they travel to those locations.

Tips to Take Action Now

TIP 1: PRIORITIZE ACCESSIBILITY

Choose a location with multiple transportation options, such as bus stops and train stations, to attract clients who rely on public transit.

Start Now: Research the public transportation routes near potential locations and assess their foot traffic.

TIP 2: OPT FOR HIGH VISIBILITY

Being on a busy street or near an intersection increases the chances of walk-ins and new customers.

Start Now: Walk through potential areas during peak times to evaluate how many people or cars pass by.

TIP 3: LEVERAGE NEARBY BUSINESSES AND SCHOOLS

Locate near popular businesses, restaurants, and schools that naturally draw people to the area.

Start Now: Identify neighborhoods with thriving businesses and schools, and consider running targeted specials to attract these crowds.

TIP 4: DON'T SKIMP ON RENT FOR THE WRONG LOCATION

It's worth paying a little more for a prime location with consistent foot traffic and visibility.

Start Now: Compare the cost difference between side street locations and high-traffic areas. Calculate the potential revenue boost from better visibility.

HOW TO START TAKING ACTION TODAY

Choosing the right location is one of the most critical decisions for a Barber or Barber shop owner. Prioritize areas with high visibility, accessibility, and natural foot traffic from nearby businesses, schools, or transit. Conduct research, observe neighborhoods at different times of day, and ask potential clients how they discover new shops. By following this checklist and focusing on visibility and accessibility, you'll set your shop up for long-term success.

Chapter 12
Hiring Barbers Who Help You Make More Money, Not Less!

Running a barbershop comes with its challenges, and one of the most significant is hiring the right barbers. The people you bring into your shop can either contribute to its success or create unnecessary headaches. This chapter delves into the true costs of hiring the wrong individuals, the importance of a proper screening process, and the strategies for maintaining a strong, effective team.

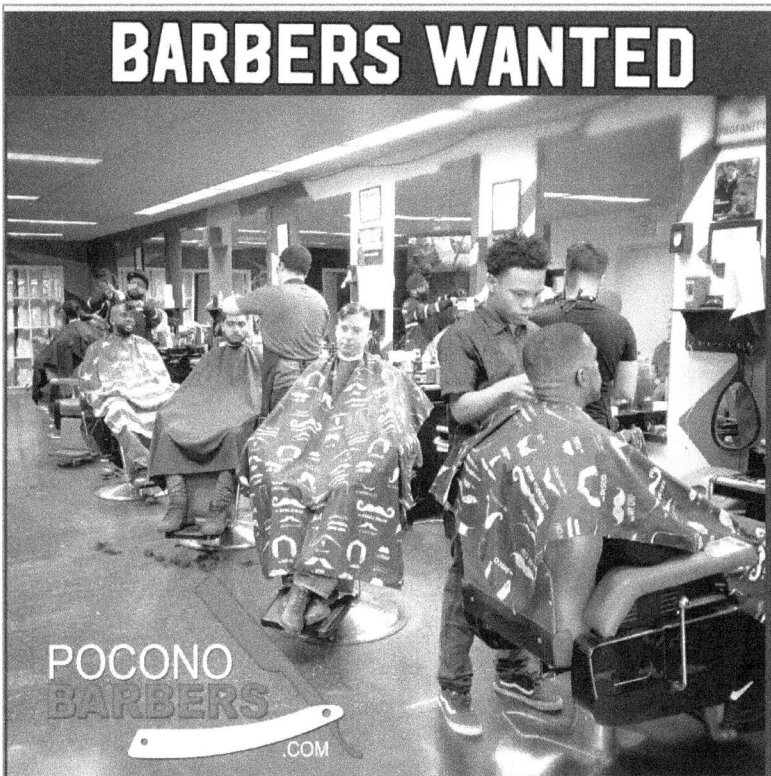

THE COST OF HIRING THE WRONG BARBERS

Over the years, I've hired more than 80 to 90 barbers, and the truth is, the majority didn't work out. While some were incredible assets to my business, others brought problems that outweighed their contributions. Hiring the wrong barber can lead to a loss of business, wasted time, and even a damaged reputation.

I've dealt with barbers who showed up late, made endless excuses, and even engaged in behavior that tarnished the image of my shop. From addicts to thieves, I've seen it all. These lessons weren't easy, but they taught me the importance of setting higher standards and being more intentional about who I brought into my shop. One particular hire stands out—a person I hired on the spot, against my better judgment. Within 15 minutes, I had to fire them. That experience reaffirmed the need for a solid hiring process.

Despite the challenges, I've also had success stories. My brother, along with a few other long-term barbers, stayed with me for years, and we made good money together. These individuals were dedicated, reliable, and easy to work with. Finding people like this takes effort, but the rewards are well worth it.

DEVELOPING A SCREENING PROCESS

One of the most valuable lessons I learned was the importance of screening potential barbers. Early in my career, I lacked a structured process, but later, I established a system that helped me identify better candidates. For starters, I implemented a two-contact rule. If a barber didn't reach out at least twice, I didn't bother pursuing them further. This simple rule helped weed out those who weren't serious or motivated.

Having applicants fill out an application form became another essential part of my process. The application gave me insight into their job history, school background, and general consistency. It's one thing to hear someone say they've worked at several shops, but seeing their employment history written down paints a clearer picture. If someone listed multiple jobs with short tenures or couldn't provide any references, those were red flags.

That said, I've also taken chances on new barbers without much experience. Some of the best team members I've had were people I trained from scratch. They often showed loyalty and stayed with me for years, which speaks to the value of investing in people willing to learn.

WORKING WITH NEW BARBERS

Even when the shop was full, I always kept a "Help Wanted" sign in the window. This strategy served two purposes: it kept the current barbers on their toes, and it ensured I had a pool of potential hires if someone left unexpectedly.

When bringing in a new barber, I would start them on a weekday rather than during the weekend rush. This gave me time to observe their skills and work ethic without the pressure of a busy shop. I also placed every new hire on a probationary period, typically lasting 60 days. During this time, I could assess their punctuality, dedication, and overall fit within the team.

Training new barbers was another approach that paid off. When you teach someone, you build a sense of reciprocity. They're more likely to stay loyal because you invested in their growth. Many of the barbers I trained stayed with me for significant periods before branching out on their own.

PROTECTING YOUR BUSINESS

As much as I valued my barbers, I learned the hard way that protecting my business was equally important. One of the best ways to do this is through an independent contractor agreement. This document outlines the expectations and responsibilities of the barber while also including a non-compete clause. For example, a barber could agree not to open a competing shop within a certain radius or time frame after leaving my shop. This measure safeguarded my business from losing clients to a barber who decided to set up shop just a few blocks away.

I'd recommend having an attorney review your independent contractor agreements to ensure they're enforceable and tailored to your specific needs. *(Free Samples at BarbershopCashFlow.com)*

MAINTAINING COMMUNICATION WITH YOUR TEAM

Regular communication is crucial for keeping the team aligned and addressing issues before they escalate. Early in my career, I didn't hold regular meetings, and the lack of structure led to chaos. Later, I introduced weekly and monthly meetings to discuss goals, shop updates, and any concerns. These meetings gave everyone a chance to voice their opinions and allowed me to resolve issues proactively.

One memorable situation involved two barbers in my shop who constantly argued. The only time they seemed to get along was when they took breaks to smoke together. While their behavior was unprofessional, they were loyal workers who showed up on time and delivered quality cuts. Ultimately, I had to balance their quirks with the value they brought to the shop. However, when barbers started costing me money or affecting the shop's reputation, it was time for them to go.

BUILDING A STRONG TEAM

To avoid hiring pitfalls, I also made it a point to build relationships with local barber schools. Many schools offer job placement services, which can connect you with aspiring barbers eager to prove themselves. This approach not only provides you with fresh talent but also strengthens your ties to the community.

Creating a positive work environment and maintaining clear communication are key to retaining good barbers. When everyone is on the same page, the shop runs smoothly, and customers notice the difference. By setting clear expectations, investing in your team, and protecting your business, you can build a barbershop that thrives for years to come.

Chapter 13
The 3 Business Skills
Every Money-Making Barber Needs

MONEY MANAGEMENT SKILLS

Managing your money is one of the most critical skills you need to succeed as a barber or shop owner. The barbering industry often runs on cash transactions, which makes it tempting—and easy—to spend recklessly. For years, when I was younger, I made a lot of mistakes with my money. I would blow it, knowing I could just make more the next day. That mindset of "I'll make it back tomorrow" led to missed opportunities for real financial growth and stability.

Let me share a story from my early days that taught me the value of money management. My brother and I found ourselves in legal trouble after a misunderstanding with a cab driver. The police accused us of theft, but when it came time to prove our innocence, we brought in our detailed bookkeeping. We had records showing where every dollar came from, down to the haircuts. Those books saved us, proving that the money was legitimately earned. That experience stayed with me forever. It reinforced how crucial it is to track your income and expenses.

Good bookkeeping isn't just about staying out of trouble—it opens doors. When I bought my first home, I only had to put down about $7,000 because my meticulous records proved my financial reliability. Without those records, getting approved would have been far harder. If you don't have the skills or tools to keep your own books, hire an accountant or invest in bookkeeping software.

Having your finances in order is what allows you to grow, pay taxes, and make major purchases.

Key Lesson: Don't let the cash-heavy nature of barbering fool you into thinking it's all expendable. Discipline and detailed financial records will set you apart from others in the industry.

MARKETING SKILLS

Marketing is the lifeblood of any business. It's not just about fancy advertisements or social media posts—it's about how you present yourself, your shop, and the value you bring to your clients. Marketing is what draws people in, and a strong brand is what keeps them coming back.

In barbering, your marketing extends far beyond flyers and social media. It includes the vibe of your shop, the cleanliness of your station, and even how you present yourself every day. A well-groomed barber with a clean, organized workspace sends a clear message: "I'm professional, and I care about my craft." That's a form of marketing. It's also about the word-of-mouth recommendations you inspire. When someone leaves your chair and someone else asks, "Where did you get that cut?"—your work is doing the marketing for you.

Later in this book, I'll dive deeper into specific marketing strategies, but for now, understand this: Marketing is about creating a perception of value. It's how people see you and decide whether to trust you with their business.

Key Lesson: Every part of your business is marketing, from how you present yourself to how you treat your clients. Focus on creating value and spreading your brand.

LEADERSHIP SKILLS

Leadership is the glue that holds everything together. Whether you're a shop owner or a barber, your leadership sets the tone for your environment. In my career, I've seen barbershops where the lack of leadership destroyed the atmosphere. Clients and barbers alike don't want to work in chaos.

Being a leader doesn't mean barking orders—it means leading by example. When you expect punctuality and professionalism from others, you have to embody those traits yourself. There were times in my early years when I didn't handle situations well. I remember once locking a client in the shop during a dispute over payment—a mistake I made twice! Looking back, I realize how immature that was. Leadership means resolving conflicts peacefully and professionally, not escalating them.

Good leadership also means taking responsibility. Whether it's a mistake in scheduling or a miscommunication, owning up to it builds respect. It also means showing appreciation for your team. A simple "thank you" or acknowledgment of their hard work can go a long way. Encouragement is another key element of leadership. If someone on your team is struggling, guide them. I always made it a point to recognize when a barber's skills were improving or when they handled a client well. People thrive under positive reinforcement.

Key Lesson: Great leaders take responsibility, resolve conflicts quickly, and inspire their teams through appreciation and encouragement.

Tips to Take Action Now

TIP 1: TRACK EVERY DOLLAR

Money management starts with discipline and accountability. It's easy to spend cash when you're earning it daily, but poor financial habits will catch up with you.

Start Now: Open a business bank account and begin tracking every dollar you earn and spend. Use software or hire an accountant to help you stay on top of your finances. Set aside money for taxes and future investments.

TIP 2: MAKE EVERY INTERACTION A MARKETING OPPORTUNITY

Marketing isn't just about flashy ads—it's about how you present yourself and your shop every day. Every client who walks through your door should leave with a reason to recommend you to others.

Start Now: Evaluate your shop and personal presentation. Is your station clean and organized? Do clients feel welcomed and valued? Take small steps to enhance the experience you provide.

TIP 3: LEAD BY EXAMPLE

Whether you're a shop owner or a barber, leadership is about setting the standard. From resolving conflicts to showing appreciation, your behavior sets the tone for your team and clients.

Start Now: Commit to leading by example. Address issues calmly and professionally, show gratitude to your team, and encourage their growth. Remember, good leadership builds trust and respect.

Chapter 14
Big Goals, Big Money: Setting Your Barbering Targets

Setting clear, measurable goals in the barber business is essential to your success. In this chapter, we'll talk about how to build a loyal clientele, set weekly haircut goals, and save $20,000 as an opportunity fund. These strategies will help you grow your business, prepare for unexpected opportunities, and stay ahead in the game.

BUILDING A LOYAL CLIENTELE BASE

Your journey begins with building a small, loyal clientele. It's crucial to have a consistent group of customers who return to you regularly. Even if you're just starting out, focus on getting 10 loyal clients. Don't worry too much about how much they pay you initially—even offer free cuts if needed. These early customers will become the foundation of your reputation.

When I first started, my loyal base included friends from the neighborhood like Oscar, Cedric, and Greg. Week after week, they came to me, and I built a solid foundation. These were the people who supported me as I refined my skills and built my business. Never forget the ones who supported you early on. They'll help you grow and spread the word about your services.

Once you've secured your first 10 loyal clients, the next goal is to expand to 50, and eventually 100. By the time you have 100 loyal clients, your reputation will be strong, and you'll have a steady stream of income. Here's the math: If you're charging $20 per cut and your 100 loyal clients each visit you just once a month, that's $2,000 a month in income. At $25 per cut, it's $2,500 a month.

WEEKLY HAIRCUT GOALS

In the beginning, you might only be doing 15–20 haircuts a week, which is common for new barbers. I remember my early days, cutting just a few heads per day and making ends meet. However, your goal should be to increase your weekly cuts steadily until you're hitting at least 125 haircuts per week.

Here's how it breaks down:

- **Friday and Saturday:** These are your busiest days. Aim to do 30–35 cuts per day. That's 60–70 cuts over the weekend.
- **Thursday:** A strong pre-weekend day, with 20–25 cuts.
- **Monday, Tuesday, Wednesday:** These days are slower, but you can still get 15–20 cuts total over the three days.

If you're averaging $20 per cut, 125 weekly haircuts equal $2,500 per week. At $25 per cut, that's $3,125 per week. This income adds up quickly, and with good money management, you'll be able to reinvest in yourself and your business.

For shop owners, the goal should be even higher. A four-chair shop should aim for 400–500 cuts per week, which translates to significant income. If you're earning $5 per cut as commission, that's $2,000–$2,500 per week from your barbers' work alone, not including your own cuts.

SETTING FINANCIAL GOALS: SAVE $20,000

Why $20,000? Most barbers don't have a clear financial target, but having one can give you focus and purpose. This $20,000 serves as your **opportunity fund**. Whether it's opening your own shop, buying equipment, or investing in property, this fund ensures you're ready when opportunity knocks.

Here's how to do it:
- Set aside $110 per week in a dedicated savings account.
- Over 3.5 years (182 weeks), you'll have $20,020.

Discipline is key. Treat this savings goal as non-negotiable. Think of it as your safety net, not just for opportunities but also for emergencies, health issues, or investments in your future.

KEY STRATEGIES FOR SUCCESS

1. **Track Your Progress:** Count every haircut you do for the week. Identify slow days and strategize ways to boost traffic during those times. For instance, offer promotions on Mondays and Tuesdays to attract more clients.
2. **Conservative Growth Goals:** Aim for a 5% increase in your weekly cuts. If you did 100 cuts this week, set a goal for 105 next week, and so on. This steady growth will add up over time.
3. **Plan for Opportunities:** When I opened my second shop, I made the rent ($1,700) in just over a week, thanks to strong community awareness. Before the shop was even ready to open, I put a "Coming Soon" sign in the window. By the time we officially opened, people were already lining up.
4. **Think Long-Term:** Saving for an opportunity fund is just the start. Use your earnings to invest in retirement accounts, real estate, or other ventures. Remember, barbering doesn't come with a 401(k)—you have to create your own financial stability.

Tips to Take Action Now

TIP 1: BUILD A STRONG FOUNDATION

Your first 10 clients are your most important. These are the people who will stick with you as you grow. Treat them like gold, and they'll help spread the word about your skills.

Start Now: Reach out to friends, family, or neighbors and offer free or discounted cuts to build your base. Focus on delivering excellent service so they keep coming back.

TIP 2: SET WEEKLY HAIRCUT GOALS

Consistency is key in this business. Track your progress and push yourself to increase your weekly cuts. Even small improvements can lead to big results over time.

Start Now: Count every haircut this week and set a realistic goal for next week. Adjust your schedule to maximize your busiest days and fill slower times with promotions or walk-ins.

TIP 3: CREATE YOUR OPPORTUNITY FUND

Saving $20,000 might sound daunting, but with discipline and a clear plan, it's achievable. This fund will give you the freedom to act on opportunities when they arise.

Start Now: Open a dedicated savings account and commit to depositing $110 every week. Treat it like a non-negotiable bill, and watch your fund grow over time.

By setting clear goals for your clientele, weekly performance, and financial future, you'll position yourself for long-term success in the barbering industry. Stay disciplined, track your progress, and always think ahead. The opportunities are endless when you're prepared.

Chapter 15
Rent or Own? The Barbershop Decision That Changes Everything

When you're building a barbershop business, one of the biggest decisions you'll face is whether to **rent** or **own** the property for your shop. Both options have their benefits and drawbacks, and the choice depends on your current position, future plans, and available resources. In this chapter, we'll explore the pros and cons of renting versus owning and share insights based on real experiences to help you make the best decision.

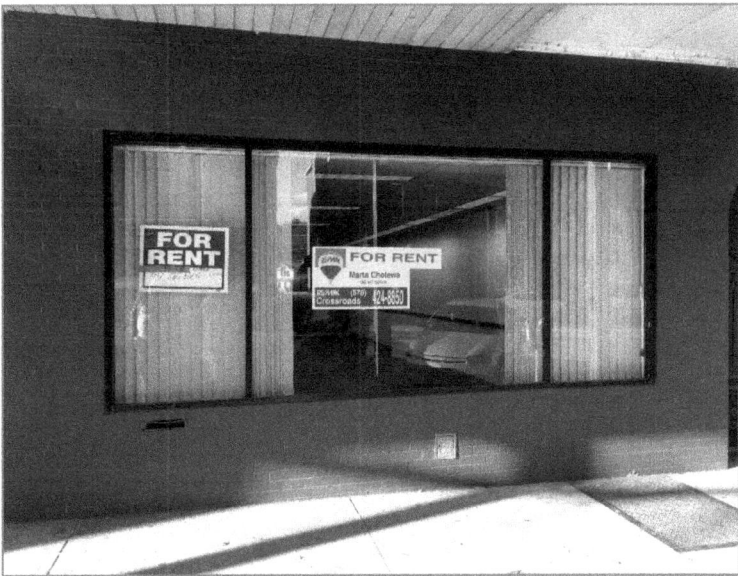

THE BENEFITS OF RENTING

Renting can offer flexibility, especially when you're just starting out. Here are the key benefits:

1. **Lower Commitment:** Renting allows you to test the waters without being tied to a long-term investment. Leases typically run for 3–5 years, giving you the chance to evaluate the location and your business performance before making a bigger commitment.

2. **Landlord Responsibilities:**
   When you rent, maintenance and repairs on the property are typically the landlord's responsibility. This means less stress for you when it comes to structural issues, major repairs, or general upkeep.

3. **Negotiable Terms:**
   Rental agreements can often be tailored to suit your needs. For example, you might negotiate options like a gross lease (where expenses like property taxes and insurance are included) or a fixed lease (where your rent remains steady for the duration of the lease). Fixed leases, in particular, are great because they protect you from rising rent costs during the lease term.

   When I opened my first shop, I had a **net lease**, where I paid $1,470 a month plus my share of property taxes and insurance. Over time, the rent escalated to $1,700, but I renegotiated with the landlord to keep the increase manageable. Flexibility like this is a huge benefit of renting.

4. **Options for Growth:**
   Many leases include **renewal options**, which allow you to extend your lease at a predetermined rate. This protects you from sudden rent hikes and gives you the flexibility to stay in a location if business is good.

When you're just starting out, options like these give you breathing room as you build your clientele.

THE DOWNSIDES OF RENTING

While renting has its advantages, there are some significant drawbacks to consider:

1. **Lack of Ownership:**
   When you rent, all the money you pay goes to the landlord, building their equity—not yours. After years of paying rent, you have no property to show for it. For example, in my second shop, I paid close to $2,000 a month. Over five years, that's $120,000—money that could have been invested in owning a property.

2. **No Control Over the Property:**
   As a tenant, you're limited in what you can do with the space. Landlords often impose restrictions on signage, renovations, or even the colors you can paint the walls. These limitations can stifle your creativity and brand expression.

3. **Uncertainty at Lease End:**
   One of the biggest risks of renting is that your lease might not be renewed. Even with renewal options, landlords can decide not to renew or significantly increase your rent. Imagine building a thriving business only to be forced out because your landlord wants to repurpose the space or charge a higher rate.

THE BENEFITS OF OWNING

Owning your property is the ultimate goal for many barbershop owners. Here's why it's worth considering:

1. **Building Equity:**

   Every payment you make on a mortgage builds equity in the property. Over time, the value of the property can increase, giving you a valuable asset. Instead of paying a landlord, you're investing in your future. For example, my friend Ty owns **Millennium Cuts** in Queens, New York. He initially rented the shop from an older owner, but after a few years, he negotiated a deal to buy the building. Now, instead of paying rent, Ty is building wealth for himself—and his property has significantly appreciated in value.

2. **Larger Cash Flow:**

   Once you pay off the mortgage, you'll have more money to reinvest in your business or save for other opportunities. Even if you're still paying off a loan, owning typically offers better long-term financial benefits than renting.

3. **Full Control:**

   When you own the property, you're the boss. Want to remodel? Go ahead. Need a bigger sign? No problem. You're only limited by local regulations, not a landlord's rules.

4. **Tax Benefits:**

   Owning a property comes with tax advantages, including depreciation deductions and the ability to write off interest on your mortgage. These benefits can make a big difference in your overall financial picture.

THE DOWNSIDES OF OWNING

While owning has significant advantages, it's not without challenges:

1. **Greater Responsibility:**
   As the owner, you're responsible for all maintenance, repairs, and improvements. From fixing the roof to upgrading plumbing, these costs can add up—especially in older buildings.

2. **Higher Initial Costs:**
   Purchasing a property requires a substantial upfront investment. Between the down payment, closing costs, and potential renovations, it can take years to save enough to buy.

3. **Market Risks:**
   If the area where you purchase a property declines in value, you could end up with a devalued asset. That's why it's crucial to carefully research locations before buying.

A PERSONAL PERSPECTIVE

When I reflect on my experience with my second shop, I can't help but think about how much money I poured into rent. At nearly $2,000 a month, I could have been paying off a mortgage and building equity. However, renting was the right decision for me at the time because it offered flexibility as I established my business.

If you're considering owning, take the time to evaluate your financial situation, business goals, and market conditions. In the long run, ownership can offer stability and wealth-building opportunities that renting simply cannot.

Tips to Take Action Now

TIP 1: EVALUATE YOUR FINANCIAL READINESS

Owning requires a significant upfront investment. Assess your savings, credit score, and financing options to determine if buying is realistic.

Start Now: If owning is a goal, begin building an opportunity fund (like we discussed in Chapter 14) to cover the down payment and closing costs.

TIP 2: NEGOTIATE LEASE TERMS

If renting is your best option, make sure to negotiate terms that protect your business. Look for fixed leases and renewal options to avoid sudden rent increases or being forced to relocate.

Start Now: Research leasing options in your area and prepare to negotiate with landlords. Don't be afraid to ask for favorable terms.

TIP 3: THINK LONG-TERM

Whether renting or owning, always keep your future goals in mind. Renting might work now, but owning could be the better option down the line. Plan for growth and make decisions that align with your vision.

Start Now: Map out a 5-year plan for your business and revisit it regularly to ensure you're on track to achieve your goals.

In the next chapter, we'll dive deeper into negotiating with landlords to ensure you get the best possible deal when renting a space.

Chapter 16
Negotiating Like a Boss:
The Deal That Sets You Up for Success

When it comes to securing a space for your barbershop, negotiating the terms of your lease or ownership deal is one of the most critical steps. The way you handle this can significantly affect your profitability, stability, and long-term success. In this chapter, we'll dive into strategies for negotiating rent and ownership deals with landlords, and I'll share real-life stories to give you actionable insights.

NEGOTIATING RENT

When negotiating rent with a landlord, it's important to strike a balance between securing favorable terms for yourself while keeping the landlord satisfied. Here are some essential points to consider:

KEEP IT MODEST

Your landlord doesn't need to know your full financial picture. When negotiating, share only the essential information needed to demonstrate that you can pay rent reliably. There's no need to disclose how many clients you have, your awards, or your business's current success. Oversharing can backfire—if a landlord believes you're making a lot of money, they may feel justified in asking for higher rent. Instead, approach the conversation as if the landlord is doing you a favor by offering a good deal, positioning yourself as a reliable tenant they can count on.

AVOID SHORT-TERM LEASES

Be cautious about landlords offering one-year trial leases. These might seem convenient, but they often leave you vulnerable. A one-year lease gives the landlord the power to change terms after the first year, especially if they notice your business thriving. I've seen it happen—like with my friend Rob, who secured a one-year lease for his shop. Once the landlord saw Rob's success, he sent his own relatives to barber school, refused to renew Rob's lease, and opened his own shop in the same space. Avoid this trap by negotiating for longer leases, ideally starting with a five-year term with renewal options.

LEVERAGE RENEWAL OPTIONS

Negotiating renewal options is critical for protecting your future. A five-year lease with additional five-year renewal options gives you flexibility and stability. With these options in place, you won't have to worry about sudden eviction or rent hikes. Plus, a good relationship with your landlord can open the door for further negotiations, such as freezing rent increases or making accommodations if you ever need to break the lease.

Here's an example: When I needed to relocate my family to another state, I had two years left on my lease from an office I rented for my internet business. I approached my landlord, explained my situation, and offered to forfeit my security deposit if he allowed me to break the lease. He agreed, and I was able to move without any legal or financial complications. This kind of negotiation is only possible when you've established a good rapport with your landlord.

INCLUDE A FIRST RIGHT OF REFUSAL CLAUSE

One of the most valuable options you can negotiate into your lease is a **first right of refusal** for purchasing the property. This gives you the first opportunity to buy the building if the landlord decides to sell. I learned the importance of this the hard way.

In my first shop, the landlord informed me he wanted to sell the property. The building housed 13 stores, including my shop, with a rent roll of $42,000 a month. He was selling it for $3.2 million. I wanted to buy it and began forming a corporation with other tenants to pool resources. But before I could finalize my plan, the landlord sold it to a real estate mogul offering cash. If I had negotiated a first right of refusal clause, I would have had time to secure financing and potentially own a highly profitable property.

GROSS LEASE VS. NET LEASE

If possible, negotiate a **gross lease** rather than a **net lease.** A gross lease includes all expenses, such as property taxes and insurance, in your rent, whereas a net lease passes those costs to you. Fixed gross leases, where your rent remains consistent throughout the lease term, offer even greater stability and predictability.

AVOID ESCALATING LEASES

Escalating leases, where rent increases by a percentage each year, can become burdensome, especially in the early stages of your business. If the landlord insists on escalations, negotiate the lowest possible percentage—3% instead of 7%, for example—and emphasize that your business is still growing. Some landlords may waive escalations for the first year to give you a better chance of success.

NEGOTIATING OWNERSHIP

Owning your property is the ultimate goal for many barbershop owners. It offers stability, equity, and control, but it also requires careful negotiation. Here are some strategies for making ownership a reality:

LOOK FOR MOTIVATED SELLERS

Motivated sellers, such as those facing foreclosure, divorce, or relocation, are often more willing to negotiate favorable terms. These sellers may even offer owner financing, allowing you to make a small down payment and pay the rest in installments directly to them.

For example, the $6,000–$7,000 you might spend on security deposits and upfront rent for a leased property could instead serve as a down payment for a building purchase. This approach lets you start building equity right away.

CONSIDER LEASE-TO-OWN AGREEMENTS

A **lease-to-own agreement** allows you to rent a property with the option to purchase it later. In these agreements, a portion of your monthly rent goes toward the purchase price, building equity over time. For instance, if your rent is $1,500 a month, you might pay an additional $300 toward the down payment. Over five years, this would amount to $18,000, which could be used as part of your purchase financing.

MAKE A FAIR OFFER

When negotiating to buy a property, research the owner's situation and the property's market value. If the owner is in a distressed situation, such as impending foreclosure, they may be open to a quick sale at a reduced price. Be prepared to present a fair and competitive offer that meets both your needs and the seller's circumstances.

PLAN FOR LONG-TERM SUCCESS

Whether renting or owning, always think ahead. Negotiate terms that protect your business and give you room to grow. Look for opportunities to transition from renting to owning when the time is right, and always have a plan for managing your finances and building equity.

Tips to Take Action Now

TIP 1: SECURE FAVORABLE LEASE TERMS

Don't settle for short-term leases or unfavorable conditions. Negotiate for fixed rates, renewal options, and first right of refusal clauses to protect your business.

Start Now: Review lease agreements carefully and consult an attorney to ensure you're getting the best terms possible.

TIP 2: EXPLORE OWNERSHIP OPPORTUNITIES

Owning your property can provide stability and financial benefits. Look for motivated sellers and consider lease-to-own agreements to ease the transition.

Start Now: Begin researching properties in your area and building relationships with local real estate agents.

TIP 3: BE PREPARED TO WALK AWAY

Sometimes, the best negotiation tactic is knowing when to say no. Don't commit to terms that could jeopardize your business's success.

Start Now: Define your deal-breakers before entering negotiations so you can make clear, confident decisions.

In the next chapter, we'll delve into the financial planning and preparation needed to support your barbershop's growth and stability.

Chapter 17
How to Raise Money for Your Own Barbershop

Making the leap to owning your own barbershop is a big step, but one that can transform your career. Whether you're ready to take the plunge now or are just starting to think about it, this chapter will help you understand the financial side of things. I'll break down the startup costs, explore different ways to raise money, and share stories to show you how achievable this goal really is.

Owning your shop doesn't have to cost as much as you might think. With a plan in place and consistent work toward your goal, it's entirely possible to open your doors without breaking the bank. Let's get into it.

BARBERSHOP STARTUP COSTS

Let's talk about what it takes to get a shop off the ground. Here are some typical costs to consider:

- **Rent and Security Deposits:** Most landlords require the first month's rent and a security deposit. Some might ask for two months' security or even the last month's rent upfront. It depends on the landlord and their confidence in your ability to pay.
- **Furniture:** You'll need barber chairs, waiting area seating, and workstations. Whether you go for new or used, these are essential.
- **Exterior and Interior Fixtures:** Think about signs for the outside of your shop, as well as interior touches like sinks, mirrors, and cabinets.

Let me break this down with examples and numbers to give you a clear picture.

FINDING DEALS ON FURNITURE

I was scrolling through a group I'm part of, Barber Society, and came across an ad from Charlotte, NC. Someone was selling **six barber chairs for $1,000.** That's a deal. Sure, the chairs weren't brand new, but a quick reupholstery job would make them look fresh.

When I started my first shop, all our chairs were secondhand. We got them for about $100 each. The shop we took over had been left in rough shape—some chairs and equipment had been stolen. But we made it work by buying used chairs and replacing only what was necessary to get started.

If you're trying to save money, check out Craigslist or local buy-and-sell groups. Deals like that $1,000 for six chairs pop up more often than you'd think.

NEW FURNITURE COSTS

If you prefer to buy new, the cost is still reasonable. I checked eBay and Amazon and found solid barber chairs for **$279 each.** For a four-chair shop, that's $1,116 for chairs. Add in workstations, which range from $139 to $299, and you're looking at about **$1,670 for furniture.**

SIGNAGE AND OTHER COSTS

When I opened my second shop, I spent $1,600 on a new sign. It included fixtures to light it up at night, which gave the shop a professional look. That was on the higher end, though. A decent sign can cost around **$400–$500.**

For rent and security deposits, expect to pay **$2,000 upfront** if the rent is $1,000/month. Then you have minor fix-ups—like patching walls, painting, or touching up floors—and startup supplies, which might add another **$1,000.**

The Total Cost

Here's the breakdown for a basic, four-chair barbershop:

- Furniture: **$1,670**
- Signage: **$400**
- Rent and security: **$2,000**
- Miscellaneous expenses: **$1,000**

Total: $5,072

For about **$5,000,** you can set up a fully functional shop. If you save more—say, $10,000 or $20,000—you'll have a cushion for slow periods or additional expenses. But even with $5,000, you can get started and begin building your dream.

Debt-Free Funding Options

I'm a big believer in avoiding debt whenever possible. If you plan ahead and save consistently, you can fund your shop without loans. But if you need to raise money, here are a few creative ways to do it:

1. RAISE MONEY THROUGH YOUR CLIENTS

Your loyal clients are often willing to support you. Offer pre-paid services at a discount—like VIP memberships or gift cards. For example, sell packages where clients pay upfront for 10 haircuts at a lower rate.

You can also hold events or contests. I knew a barber who threw a party for his clients with a small cover charge. He used the proceeds to buy chairs and workstations for his new shop.

2. CROWDFUNDING

Platforms like **GoFundMe** can be a great way to raise money. Share your story with your clients and community, letting them know you're starting your own shop. You'd be surprised how many people are willing to chip in. Even small donations add up.

I've seen barbers raise thousands of dollars this way, often from just a few generous contributors. Someone might drop $1,000 into your campaign just to help you out.

3. SIDE HUSTLES

If you have skills outside of barbering, use them to earn extra cash. Whether it's selling products, teaching classes, or offering consultations, these side hustles can fund your shop.

Loans: Proceed With Caution

If you absolutely need to take out a loan, keep it small—no more than **$5,000.** The barbershop business is unique in that you can start small and grow gradually. For example, you can start with four chairs and add more as your business expands.

Partners: A Word of Warning

While partnerships can work, they're not my personal preference. I've always run my shops solo because I value having full control. That said, I know barbers who've successfully partnered with others to split costs and responsibilities. If you go this route, make sure you and your partner are aligned on your vision and financial goals.

FINAL THOUGHTS

Starting your own barbershop doesn't have to cost a fortune. With about **$5,000,** you can set up a solid foundation. By planning ahead, saving consistently, and exploring creative ways to raise funds, you can achieve your dream without taking on unnecessary debt.

In the next chapter, we'll dive into marketing strategies to help you grow your barbershop or build your clientele if you're just starting out.

Tips to Take Action Now

TIP 1: CALCULATE YOUR STARTUP COSTS

Starting a barbershop might be more affordable than you think. By carefully planning for furniture, rent, signage, and other expenses, you can estimate exactly how much money you'll need.

Start Now: Write out a list of everything your shop will require, including chairs, workstations, and signage. Compare prices for new and used items, and calculate a realistic budget. Aim for around **$5,000** as your starting point.

TIP 2: BUILD A SAVINGS PLAN

The best way to fund your shop is debt-free. By saving a small amount each week, you can reach your goal in 1–3 years. Consistent effort makes it possible.

Start Now: Open a dedicated savings account for your barbershop fund. Commit to setting aside a specific amount each week, whether it's $50, $75, or $100. Stick to the plan, and watch your savings grow.

TIP 3: USE CREATIVE FUNDING METHODS

Your clients and community can help you raise the money you need. By offering pre-paid services, hosting events, or using crowdfunding platforms, you can gather support to fund your shop.

Start Now: Brainstorm ways to involve your clients. Could you sell discounted haircut packages or host a community event? Set a specific goal—like raising $5,000—and start promoting your campaign to your network.

TIP 4: AVOID TAKING ON DEBT

If possible, avoid loans altogether. A small loan might help, but debt can create unnecessary pressure when starting your business.

Start Now: Revisit your budget and explore all possible ways to fund your shop without borrowing money. If you absolutely must take a loan, keep it small—no more than **$5,000.**

TIP 5: PLAN FOR FLEXIBILITY

You don't need to open a fully equipped shop on day one. Start with the basics and grow your business over time.

Start Now: Focus on securing the essentials—four chairs and workstations, for example. Once your shop begins generating revenue, reinvest in upgrades and additional equipment.

These tips should align with the actionable advice you're sharing throughout the book and match the format we've established for other chapters. Let me know if they work for you!

Chapter 18
30 Game-Changing Tips for Barber Success

30 Barbershop Tips to Grow Your Clientele

Let me start by saying this: these tips are **not in any particular order**. Don't think of them as a step-by-step process. They're simply tools to help you grow your business. Pick the ones that resonate with you and apply them in your shop. With that being said, let's get into it.

1. TUESDAYS AND WEDNESDAYS DISCOUNTS

When I first opened my shop, Tuesdays and Wednesdays were always the slowest days of the week. I decided to do something about that. I made a big yellow sign—it was hard to miss—that said, **"Discount Haircuts on Tuesdays and Wednesdays."** That one move brought in more students, people passing by, and new customers who just wanted to take advantage of the deal. Over time, those discounted days turned into regular business days with a steady flow of customers.

2. SUNDAY AND MONDAY TRAFFIC

Sunday and Monday? Those are the days I noticed a steady stream of **new customers**. Why? Because most barbershops were closed on those days. Customers would see my shop open when their usual spot wasn't, and they'd give me a try. Many of them became regulars who started coming back throughout the week or on weekends. Staying open when others are closed is a smart move if you want to grow your clientele.

3. OPEN EARLY, STAY LATE

If you're trying to build a customer base, you have to put in the hours. I'd open my shop an hour earlier than the competition and stay open an hour later. That made a big difference. For example, there was this Barber named Freddie who cut Anthony Mason's hair back when he played for the Knicks. Freddie's shop was popular and just one block away from my shop. He didn't open up shop until 11:00 AM. However, I would open by 9:30 AM, and we'd catch some of their overflow, especially from people who didn't want to wait or didn't even realize Freddie's wasn't open yet. One of my barbers, Rasheed, one morning cut Jason Williams 'who played for the NBA Nets. He was looking to get a cut early at Freddie's shop and they were not open yet. Rasheed didn't even realize it was him until he was done. He gave him $70 for the haircut.

4. SET STRATEGIC PRICING

When I opened my second shop, I knew I had to stand out. Other shops in the area were charging $12 to $15 for a cut, sometimes more for a razor lineup. So, I decided to charge **$8 every day.** That price? It filled up my shop—even on slow days. Some customers tipped extra, knowing they were still paying less than they would at another shop. At the end of the day, my barbers were happy because they stayed busy, and we built a reputation as the go-to spot.

5. SPEED UP YOUR CUTS

Time is money in this business. If you can cut hair in **15 minutes or less**, you'll be able to serve more clients and make more money. It's that simple. The key is to get efficient without sacrificing quality. Once you master this, you'll see how it impacts your bottom line.

6. WORK WITH BETTER BARBERS

Here's something I learned: **iron sharpens iron.** When I worked with barbers who were better than me, it pushed me to step up my game. For example, when my brother and I worked together, we were always trying to outdo each other. It made both of us better. Later, at my second shop, I hired a guy named Martin who used to work at Freddie's. He wasn't the most skilled Barber, but he was **fast.** He could knock out a haircut in 10 minutes, and his speed challenged me to move faster while maintaining quality. If you surround yourself with talented barbers, it will improve your game.

7. BE WILLING TO MOVE

If your location isn't bringing in the traffic you need, don't be afraid to relocate. Sometimes, the best move you can make for your business is to go where the customers are. If that means saving up and moving to a busier area, it's worth considering.

8. SPECIALS AND REFERRAL PROGRAMS

I've tried all kinds of specials—Father-and-Son discounts, "Bring 3, Get 1 Free," and even referral programs. For example, with referrals, I'd offer a free haircut or a discount to customers who brought in new clients. These promotions not only attract new people but also encourage your regulars to spread the word about your shop.

9. GIVE MORE THAN WHAT'S PAID FOR

Here's a simple way to build loyalty: **over-deliver.** If you normally charge extra for a razor lineup, throw it in for free once in a while and let the client know. Say, "Hey, I usually charge $5 for the razor, but I'll include it today since you brought in your brother." Little gestures like that go a long way in building trust and loyalty.

10. LEVERAGE BIG WINDOWS

In both my first and second shops, I had big windows that faced the street. Why? Because they drew in walk-ins. People standing outside could see the barbers in action, which piqued their curiosity. If you're looking for a location, try to find one with a large, visible storefront.

11. CONSISTENCY IS KEY

If you say your shop opens at 9:00 AM, be there at 9:00 AM. Customers value reliability. If they show up and you're not there, they'll go somewhere else. Don't give your competition an edge because you weren't consistent.

12. GET ONLINE

If you don't have a **Facebook Fan Page** or **Instagram**, you're missing out on a huge opportunity. Social media is where your clients are, so you need to meet them there. Post your best haircuts, engage with followers, and build an online presence. Also, invest in a website. Make sure it's optimized for local searches like "Barbers near me."

13. ALWAYS ASK HOW CLIENTS FOUND YOU

This is one of the simplest ways to know what's working. Did they find you on Instagram? Through a friend? On Google? Use this feedback to focus your marketing efforts on what's driving traffic to your shop.

14. KEEP STUDYING YOUR CRAFT

You can't stop learning in this business. The more you know, the better you'll be. I remember going to the library as a teenager and checking out books on barbering. I wanted to master every style and technique. Even now, I'm always looking for ways to improve. You should do the same.

15. GIVE BACK TO THE COMMUNITY

Every now and then, offer free haircuts. Whether it's for kids going back to school or people in need, giving back creates goodwill and strengthens your reputation. Plus, it just feels good to help others.

16. BUSINESS CARDS AND FLYERS STILL WORK

Not everyone is on social media, so don't underestimate the power of **business cards** and **flyers.** Hand them out everywhere—at malls, events, and even on the street. Make sure they include all your contact information and social media handles.

17. A BONUS TIP: NEVER STOP HUSTLING

This business is all about hustle. Whether it's handing out flyers, posting on Instagram, or staying late to catch one last client, you have to put in the work. Success doesn't come to those who wait—it comes to those who go out and get it.

18. OFFER LOYALTY PUNCH CARDS

Create a "Buy 5 Haircuts, Get 1 Free" punch card. This simple program encourages repeat business and builds loyalty.

19. BARBERSHOP MERCHANDISE

Sell branded merchandise like t-shirts, hats, or grooming products. Clients wearing your gear promote your shop wherever they go.

20. HOST THEMED EVENTS

Organize events like "College Night" or "Military Appreciation Days" to attract specific groups of clients and boost visibility.

21. PARTNER WITH LOCAL BUSINESSES

Collaborate with gyms, clothing stores, or tattoo shops. Offer discounts to their customers in exchange for them promoting your shop.

22. CREATE A "BARBER OF THE WEEK" FEATURE

Highlight one of your barbers every week on social media, showcasing their work and story. It builds trust and personal connection with clients.

23. POST BEFORE-AND-AFTER PHOTOS

Showcase transformations on Instagram or Facebook. These photos grab attention and act as proof of your skill.

24. OFFER FIRST-TIME CUSTOMER DEALS

Give a small discount to first-time clients to get them through the door. If you impress them, they'll return.

25. RUN LIMITED-TIME PROMOTIONS

Create urgency with promotions like, "$5 off haircuts for the first 20 customers this Saturday!"

26. START A YOUTUBE CHANNEL

Share haircut tutorials, grooming tips, or shop highlights. This establishes your expertise and brings new attention to your shop.

27. CREATE REFERRAL CONTESTS

Reward clients for referrals with contests like, "Refer the most friends this month and win free haircuts for a year."

28. OFFER GROUP DISCOUNTS

Provide deals for groups, like wedding parties, sports teams, or office employees looking to come in together.

29. USE TEXT MESSAGE MARKETING

Send text reminders about appointments, specials, or slow-day discounts. SMS marketing keeps your shop top of mind.

30. GROOMING PACKAGES

Offer bundled services like haircuts, beard trims, and hot towel shaves at a slight discount. Packages encourage clients to spend more.

31. SPONSOR LOCAL SPORTS TEAMS

Sponsor jerseys or gear for local youth sports teams. Your shop's name on their uniforms is free advertising.

32. RUN HOLIDAY PROMOTIONS

33. Around holidays like Christmas or Father's Day, offer gift cards or "Father & Son" haircut specials to attract families.

CONCLUSION

These strategies, along with the bonus tips, are designed to help you build your clientele, grow your reputation, and achieve your goals. Take them to heart and put them into practice

Chapter 19
Making Money Beyond the Barbershop

This chapter is all about expanding your income streams beyond cutting hair. We'll focus on three main areas:

1. **Products and Services** – How you can create and sell products or services that work for you after they're created.

2. **The Potential in the Beauty Industry** – Exploring the opportunities within the beauty, Barber, and skincare industries.

3. **Growing Your Audience** – Leveraging social media, mailing lists, and other tools to grow your presence and influence.

Let's get into it.

1. PRODUCTS AND SERVICES

When you create your own products or services, you're setting yourself up for income that doesn't rely on you cutting someone's hair one-on-one. Think about it—every haircut requires your time and effort. That's fine, but there's a limit to how many heads you can cut in a day. Products and services allow you to **leverage your time** and scale your income.

Here's how it works:

- You identify a **problem or need** in your industry.
- You create a solution, package it, and market it.
- Once your product is in the market, it starts working for you.

For example, if you're constantly struggling with a specific type of fade, maybe you could design a Clipper attachment that makes it easier to blend. Think about it—at some point, someone sat down and said, "Let's put a lever on Clippers so barbers can adjust the blades without switching attachments." That idea turned into a standard feature, and whoever invented it is probably still making money from that patent.

Key Tip:

When you experience a problem in your shop, don't assume you're the only one. Chances are, thousands of other barbers are dealing with the same issue, and a product that solves it could be your ticket to wealth.

Take **wall Clippers**, for example. The founders didn't sell their products one-by-one to every barber in the world—they created a product, patented it, and let the product do the work. Now, their brand services professionals, amateurs, and even parents cutting their kids' hair at home.

2. THE POTENTIAL IN THE BEAUTY INDUSTRY

The beauty and Barber industry is massive. In the U.S. alone, it generated **$56.2 billion** in 2015. Globally, the numbers are even bigger. This is why I encourage you to think about how you can tap into this market beyond the chair.

Let me give you an example. Back in 1999, a friend of mine named Sean and I came up with an idea for a health insurance plan specifically for barbers. At the time, barbers didn't have many affordable healthcare options, and we thought, "What if we created a plan where barbers could pay $40 or $50 a month for coverage?" It would've been a game-changer.

Now, we never executed that idea, but the point is, if we had launched it, it could've helped thousands of barbers while generating consistent income for us. Always think about what's missing in the industry and how you can fill that gap.

FLEX RAZOR EXAMPLE

Let me tell you about my friend Rob Jones. He created a product called the **Flex Razor**, which is now in thousands of barbershops. Here's how it happened:

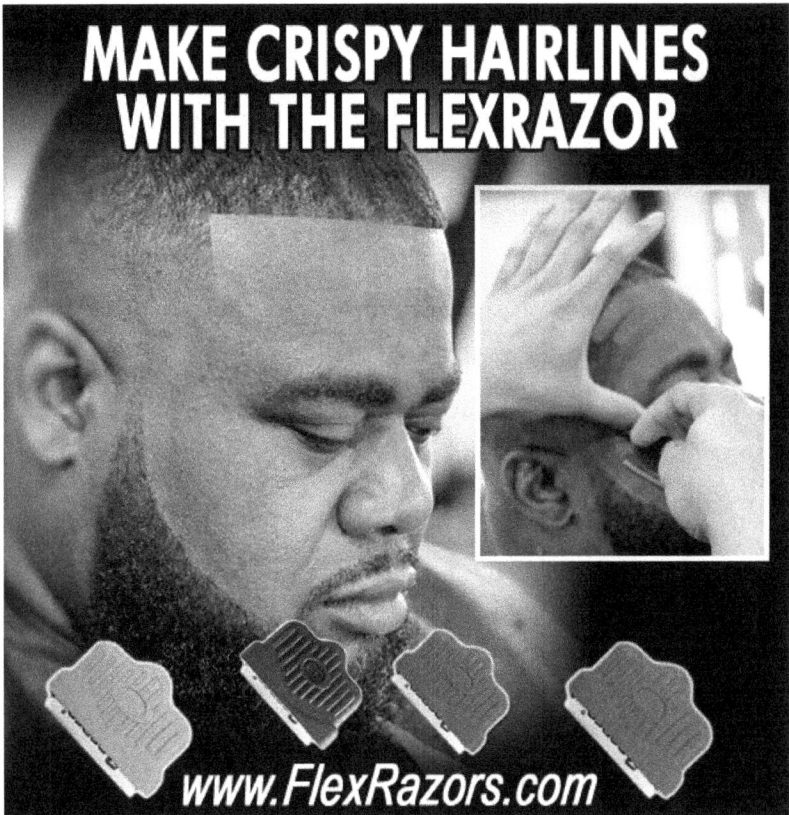

Rob noticed that he could get sharper lines using a bent double-edge blade, but a customer once told him, "That doesn't look professional." That feedback pushed him to create a tool that gave him the same results but looked professional. He developed the Flex Razor, got it manufactured, and started selling it.

Now, the Flex Razor isn't for everyone, just like not every Barber prefers the same Clipper. But for those who use it, it's a game-changer. The key takeaway here is that Rob turned a problem into a product that now generates income for him while he sleeps.

3. GROWING YOUR AUDIENCE

Social media has completely changed the game for barbers. Back when I started, we didn't have Facebook, Instagram, or YouTube. Everything was word-of-mouth, Flyers, and business cards. But now, with platforms like **YouTube** and **Instagram**, you can build a following that extends far beyond your local shop.

Many other barbers with huge followings and millions of views.

Many barbers are doing more than cutting hair—they're **building brands.** Some of them get sponsorships, free products, or affiliate deals with companies like Amazon. For example, if a new Clipper comes out, they can review it, include an Amazon link, and earn commissions every time someone buys through their link.

Tip:

If you want to build your brand, start with the basics:
- Create a **YouTube channel** and post tutorials or reviews.
- Start an **Instagram page** to showcase your cuts.
- Create a **Facebook fan page** to connect with your clients and local community.

- Always include your contact info and social media handles on your Flyers, business cards, and shop materials.

MAILING LISTS

One of the most valuable tools you can have is a **mailing list.** Social media platforms are great, but they can change their algorithms or even shut down tomorrow. With a mailing list, you control your audience and can reach them directly whenever you want.

For example, let's say you're launching a new product or offering a discount at your shop. A mailing list allows you to send that information directly to your clients or followers, ensuring they see it.

OPPORTUNITIES ARE EVERYWHERE

With the growth of the internet and social media, there are more opportunities than ever to make money in this industry. Whether it's creating a product, launching a service, or building your brand online, the possibilities are endless.

Here's what I recommend:

1. Think about the problems you encounter daily and how you can solve them.
2. Use social media to grow your influence and reach.
3. Build a mailing list to stay connected with your audience.
4. Look for ways to monetize beyond the chair—whether that's through products, affiliate marketing, or consulting.

FINAL THOUGHTS

This chapter is about showing you the bigger picture. The barbershop is your foundation, but don't let it limit you. Think beyond the chair. Whether it's creating products, building a brand, or offering services, there's a world of opportunities waiting for you.

Tips to Take Action Now

TIP 1: START WITH A PRODUCT OR SERVICE YOU KNOW WELL

Creating a product or service beyond cutting hair is easier when it's connected to your daily experience in the barbershop. Look for tools or products you already use but feel could be improved.

Start Now:

- Think of something you use daily that could be made better.
- Is there a common product your clients ask for? Start there.
- Research suppliers or manufacturers who can help bring your idea to life.

TIP 2: BUILD A MAILING LIST TO STAY CONNECTED

A mailing list lets you stay in touch with clients and potential customers for your products or services. It's a direct way to share updates, promotions, or new offerings.

Start Now:

- Create a simple form on a website or a physical signup sheet in your shop.
- Offer a small incentive like a discount on services for signing up.

- Use free tools like Mailchimp to manage your mailing list.

TIP 3: DEVELOP MULTIPLE INCOME STREAMS

Leverage your skills to build income beyond the chair. Think of products (like grooming tools) or services (like teaching or consultations) that align with your expertise.

Start Now:
- Create a small batch of a product (e.g., beard oil, pomade) and sell it in your shop.
- Record a tutorial or host a live class on a platform like Instagram or YouTube.
- Partner with brands to promote or review their products for a fee.

TIP 4: USE SOCIAL MEDIA TO GROW YOUR BRAND

Social media can amplify your business and attract new customers for your products or services. Build a strong presence with consistent, high-quality content.

Start Now:
- Post photos or videos of your work daily on Instagram.
- Include hashtags like #BarberLife or #MensGrooming to reach a broader audience.
- Share tips, tricks, or tutorials to show your expertise and build trust.

TIP 5: TAP INTO AFFILIATE MARKETING

Affiliate programs allow you to earn money by recommending products you love. When clients or other barbers buy using your link, you get a percentage of the sale.

Start Now:

- Sign up for affiliate programs like Amazon Associates or join barber-specific programs.
- Post reviews or tutorials featuring products you use and add your affiliate link.
- Share these reviews on your social media or mailing list to drive traffic.

TIP 6: FOCUS ON SOLVING A PROBLEM

The best products and services solve specific problems. Pay attention to what your clients and fellow barbers complain about—this is where opportunity lies.

Start Now:

- Keep a notebook or digital file where you jot down common problems in the barbershop.
- Brainstorm solutions that you could create or improve upon.
- Begin researching how to bring one idea to market.

TIP 7: NEVER STOP LEARNING

Growing beyond the barbershop requires staying informed about industry trends, new products, and marketing strategies.

Start Now:

- Attend industry events or trade shows.
- Take courses on product development, marketing, or entrepreneurship.
- Follow industry leaders online to stay inspired.

Chapter 20
Safety First: Protecting and Profits

WHY BARBERSHOPS ARE TARGETED

Barbershops can sometimes feel like easy targets, especially on weekends when cash flow is high. They're often seen as cash-heavy businesses where people think they can grab money and go.

Example:

I had an experience back in the day when I was 16, working late in the shop with my brother and another Barber. A guy came in as we were closing, pulled out a gun, and shot at the ceiling to make it clear he wasn't playing. He demanded cash and jewelry. At that time, I used to wear flashy jewelry, and that incident made me stop. I realized how much attention you draw when you're wearing expensive items in the shop.

Later, we found out from a neighboring shop owner that the guy had been casing the place all day. He'd been across the street, at the corner, watching us before he came in. That taught me the importance of paying attention to your surroundings and not staying isolated in the back of the shop during closing.

SECURITY CAMERAS

Back in the day, installing cameras was expensive, so I didn't think about it. Now, you can pick up a good camera system for a couple of hundred dollars. I remember seeing a fellow business owner who had cameras set up in his pizza shop. He could monitor everything from his phone in real time. That got me thinking about how much easier it is now to add that layer of security.

Example:

There was a time when employee theft was an issue. I ran a Commission-based shop, and when I wasn't there, some barbers would skip out on paying their percentage. If I'd had cameras, I could have called them out with proof instead of relying on memory. Having cameras installed at the front and back of the shop, plus by the register, can protect not only your business but also your employees and customers.

SHOP SECURITY PRECAUTIONS

Security in your shop is about staying visible and taking simple steps to avoid making yourself an easy target.

1. **Stay in the Front of the Shop:**

   If you're working late, don't sit all the way in the back. Someone could easily walk in, and if you're not visible from the door, you're giving them the opportunity to set up before you even know they're there. I learned this the hard way. It's better to stay in the front where you can see who's coming in and out.

2. **Secure the Register:**

   Your cash register should be behind a barrier or in a place where it's not immediately visible from the door. Don't leave it wide open or easily accessible. It's also a good practice to clear out cash regularly, especially before closing time.

3. **Lock the Door Late at Night:**

   If you're cutting hair late, keep the door locked and use a buzzer system to control who comes in. It's a simple step that can prevent someone from walking in and catching you off guard.

4. **Don't Allow Isolation:**

   If someone tries to isolate you, like taking you to the backroom or outside the shop, that's a big red flag. I'd always recommend negotiating to keep the situation in a visible, open area. In my experience, people who get isolated often face worse outcomes. My rule is: give them the money if they want it, but don't let them take you somewhere where they have more control.

LIFE OVER CASH

Your life is more important than the money you've made that day or week. If you're ever in a situation where someone has a weapon and demands money or valuables, give it to them. It's not worth risking your life over cash or material things.

Example:

When I was robbed, as soon as the guy fired the shot, I said, "You got it. You got it." I made sure he knew I wasn't resisting, and we handed over the cash and jewelry. He had my brother put everything in a bag and left. At the end of the day, we walked away with our lives, and that's what matters most.

VISIBLE DETERRENTS

Having cameras, visible security signs, and a well-lit shop are all deterrents. Thieves are less likely to target a shop where they know they're being recorded or where they'll be easily seen.

Example:

In one of my shops, I had a large front window, and that helped. People standing at the bus stop could see everything happening inside, which made it less likely for someone to try something. A big window also attracts walk-ins, so it's a win-win.

KEY TAKEAWAYS

- **Invest in Cameras:** They're affordable now and can protect you from theft, both from outsiders and employees. Plus, live monitoring gives you peace of mind.
- **Stay Visible:** Don't linger in the back of the shop, especially during closing hours. Stay in the front where you can see who's coming and going.
- **Secure Your Cash:** Keep the register out of sight and remove cash regularly.
- **Lock Your Doors:** Use a buzzer system during late hours to control entry.
- **Prioritize Safety:** If someone tries to rob you, comply. Your life is worth more than any material possession.

These are lessons I've learned firsthand over the years. You never think it'll happen to you until it does. Taking these precautions can make a big difference in keeping your shop, your team, and yourself safe.

Chapter 21

Keep More Cash – Pay Less Taxes: Business Structure, and the IRS

TAX WRITE-OFFS

One of the most overlooked opportunities for barbers is the power of tax write-offs. Every dollar you spend on your business can potentially reduce your taxable income. Here's a breakdown of write-offs:

- **Shop Rent and Booth Rent:** If you're paying $24,000 annually for shop rent and made $100,000, you're taxed on $76,000 after deductions.

- **Insurance:** All forms of insurance, including health, business liability, and even life insurance tied to your business, are deductible.

- **Advertising:** Flyers, cards, websites, web hosting, and promotional materials are all tax-deductible.

- **Tools and Supplies:** Clippers, chairs, alcohol, shaving products—anything used to operate your shop is deductible. Keep those receipts!

- **Educational Expenses:** Courses, seminars, and even this book are deductible because they enhance your professional skills.

- **Travel and Lodging:** If you travel to an event or even cut a client's hair in another city, you can deduct those expenses.

- **Meals with Clients:** These are partially deductible, with the percentage depending on your business structure.

- **Loans and Interest:** Interest on loans used for your business can also be deducted.

Example:

When I started in this business, I didn't realize how much I was leaving on the table by not keeping track of my expenses. One year, I wrote off everything from advertising to a new set of Clippers, which saved me thousands in taxes.

TAX SHELTERS

The wealthy don't just pay less in taxes because they earn more—they leverage tax shelters to keep more of their money. Here are a few strategies you can use:

- **IRA Contributions:** Open an IRA (Individual Retirement Account). Money you put in is non-taxable until retirement, making it a great way to save while lowering your taxable income.

- **Corporations:** Forming an LLC or S-Corporation provides tax benefits, including the ability to deduct meals, vehicles, and even health insurance under the business name.

- **Real Estate Investments:**
    1. Real estate builds wealth and shelters taxes. For example, I bought a property for $150,000. Four years later, it was worth $300,000. Instead of selling it outright, I pulled out $100,000 in equity through a loan—tax-free and then sold it. The $100,00 was tax free this way.
    2. Many wealthy individuals use real estate as a way to grow wealth while minimizing taxes.

- **Business Loans:** Loans to start or grow your shop aren't taxed as income. Use this strategy wisely to expand without heavy tax burdens.

Example:

When I took equity out of my property, I reinvested it into another business. That money wasn't taxed because it was technically a loan. This is a strategy anyone can use to grow their wealth.

BUSINESS STRUCTURE

Your business structure determines how much tax you pay and how protected you are from liability. Here are the most common structures:

LLC (LIMITED LIABILITY COMPANY):

- Protects your personal assets in case of a lawsuit.
- Allows you to write off business expenses, including vehicles and meals.
- Simple and affordable to set up. In my state, I've started LLCs for as little as $90.

Example:

When I leased a vehicle for my business, I did it through my LLC. That way, I could deduct the full cost of the lease and avoid mixing business with personal expenses.

S-CORPORATION:

- Best for businesses earning under $600,000 annually.
- Avoids double taxation (corporate and individual levels) that occurs with C-Corporations.

Example:

My first S-Corporation was for a music production company I started at 18. By structuring it this way, I avoided double taxation and took advantage of tax benefits specific to corporations.

SOLE PROPRIETORSHIP AND PARTNERSHIPS:

- Easy to set up but offer no personal liability protection.
- Not recommended for long-term growth.

KEY TAKEAWAYS

- **Track Everything:** Keep receipts for all expenses. They're your lifeline when it comes to tax season.
- **Hire an Accountant:** IRS codes change frequently. A competent accountant ensures you're compliant and maximizing deductions.
- **Start an LLC:** Even if you're just renting a booth, operating under an LLC can protect you and provide tax advantages.
- **Invest in Real Estate:** Use real estate to build wealth and shelter taxes. Borrow against equity instead of selling outright to avoid heavy tax hits.

Example:

When I was younger, I didn't think much about business structure or taxes. Now, I see the value in leveraging these tools to not just save money but build lasting wealth.

FINAL THOUGHTS

This chapter wraps up everything I've learned about taxes, business, and financial growth. As a Barber, no one's going to take care of your finances for you. You have to take control, plan ahead, and use every tool available to build your wealth.

The tools I've shared in this chapter—and throughout this course—aren't just theory. They're real strategies I've used to succeed. And as I dive back into opening a shop, I'll document the journey so you can see these strategies in action.

To Your Success!

Tips to Take Action Now

This chapter dives into essential strategies for managing taxes, leveraging tax shelters, and establishing a solid business structure. Implementing these tips will help you save money, protect your assets, and lay a strong foundation for financial growth.

TIP 1: TRACK EVERY TAX-DEDUCTIBLE EXPENSE

Ensure you document all allowable deductions, such as rent, tools, supplies, and educational courses. Keeping track of receipts and invoices can significantly lower your taxable income.

Start Now: Set up a system to log every expense related to your Barber shop. Use apps like QuickBooks or a simple spreadsheet to organize receipts and invoices.

Tip 2: Explore Tax Shelters

Take advantage of programs like IRAs (Individual Retirement Accounts) to shelter your income from taxes while saving for the future. Consider real estate as a long-term tax-efficient investment.

Start Now: Open an IRA and start contributing regularly. If you own property, speak with a financial advisor about leveraging your equity for tax advantages.

Tip 3: Choose the Right Business Structure

Operating as an LLC (Limited Liability Company) or an S Corporation offers tax advantages and shields your personal assets from liability. This structure also lets you take more deductions, such as health insurance and business-related meals.

Start Now: Research the process for forming an LLC in your state. Many states allow you to file online for as little as $100. Consult with an accountant to determine the best structure for your situation.

TIP 4: DEDUCT BUSINESS-RELATED TRAVEL

Traveling for Barber events, training, or client services can often be deducted as a business expense. Even vacations can qualify if you document business activities during your trip.

Start Now: Plan your next trip with a business purpose in mind, such as meeting a client or attending a Barber expo. Keep detailed records of your travel itinerary and expenses.

TIP 5: REINVEST IN YOUR BUSINESS

Use tax savings to upgrade your equipment, expand your shop, or explore new marketing strategies. Reinvesting helps you grow your income while reducing your tax burden.

Start Now: Identify one area of your business—such as marketing or equipment—that could use improvement. Allocate tax savings toward this investment.

HOW TO START TAKING ACTION TODAY

Managing taxes and structuring your business properly can transform your financial future. Begin by tracking every deductible expense and exploring tax shelters like IRAs. Evaluate your current business structure and upgrade to an LLC or S Corporation to unlock additional benefits. Leverage travel and other write-offs to maximize savings, and reinvest those savings into growing your Barber business. With the right approach, you can retain more of your hard-earned income while setting the stage for long-term success.

Phase 2
How I Built a Six-Figure
Barbershop in Two Years

Phase Two Introduction:
Building a 100K Barber Shop
in Less Than Two Years

Welcome to Phase Two of this book, where I take you beyond theory and dive into the real-world journey of building a thriving barbershop business. In the earlier chapters, I walked you through my career spanning the 1990s to the early 2000s. During that time, I opened and operated two successful barbershops, gaining invaluable experience. After stepping away from the industry to focus on raising my family and building a successful internet business, I thought my barbering days were behind me.

Then came 2017. While creating my first barbering course, inspired by my experiences from decades earlier, I found myself reconnected with my passion for the business. That course, originally meant to teach others, reignited a fire in me. I challenged myself: could I apply everything I was teaching and achieve success in real-time, starting from scratch? The answer was a resounding yes.

This section of the book documents my return to the industry after 15 years, showcasing how I reopened a barbershop, built a clientele from zero, and grew the business to $100,000 in annual revenue in less than two years. **Phase Two** isn't just a reflection on past lessons—it's an actionable blueprint based on what I actually did, starting in 2017, to achieve rapid success.

WHAT YOU'LL LEARN IN PHASE TWO

This book is more than a story; it's a guide. Here's what you'll gain from Phase Two:

- **The Steps I Took to Open My Third Barbershop**: Learn how I went from zero clients and no momentum to creating a flourishing business, step by step.
- **Building a Clientele from Scratch**: Discover the strategies I used to fill my chairs with loyal customers, even in a completely new location.
- **My Business Model and Management Style**: From operations to leadership, see how I structured my shop to ensure smooth operations and consistent growth.
- **My Philosophy on Business Growth**: Understand the principles I applied to scale the business quickly, while minimizing risks and maximizing profitability.

MY JOURNEY BACK TO THE BARBERING INDUSTRY

After a 15-year hiatus, my decision to return wasn't just about reopening a barbershop—it was about proving to myself that I could take everything I'd learned and apply it successfully in today's market. It wasn't an easy decision. My wife thought I was crazy, especially since I'd built a comfortable life through online ventures. But the more I worked on my 2017 course, the more I felt drawn back to the craft and the industry I'd loved for so many years.

The challenge was exciting. Could I really start from zero, build a clientele, and reach six figures in two years? This section of the book chronicles every step, from finding the right location to recruiting barbers, setting prices, and creating systems that worked.

WHAT'S COMING IN PHASE TWO

Here's an overview of the upcoming chapters in Phase Two, so you know what to expect as we move forward:

1. **The History Behind My Decision**: I'll explain the thought process and inspiration that led me to return to the barbering industry after such a long break.
2. **Researching the Market**: Learn how I analyzed the competition, assessed local demand, and identified the perfect area to set up shop.
3. **Finding and Securing the Right Location**: From negotiating lease terms to identifying high-traffic areas, I'll share my insights on picking the right spot for a barbershop.
4. **Setting Up Shop on a Budget**: Discover how I created a professional, welcoming environment without breaking the bank, focusing on resourcefulness and cost-saving strategies.
5. **Launch Strategy**: I'll break down the steps I took to ensure a successful opening that generated buzz and brought customers through the door.
6. **Pricing Strategies to Attract Clients**: Learn how I set competitive yet profitable pricing that helped me build a steady clientele quickly.
7. **Attracting and Recruiting Barbers**: From creating appealing contracts to fostering a team-oriented environment, this chapter explores my approach to finding the right barbers.
8. **Booth Rent vs. Commission**: See how I balanced these two payment models based on my market's needs and the preferences of my barbers.
9. **Creating Solid Booth Rental Agreements**: Learn how to protect your business while offering fair terms to your barbers.
10. **Appointments vs. Walk-Ins**: Understand the pros and cons of each model and how to make both work for your shop.
11. **Barbershop Management**: Get insights into creating systems and routines that ensure your shop runs smoothly.

12. **Navigating Reviews**: I'll share my experiences dealing with online reviews and how to build a positive reputation in today's digital landscape.

13. **Legal Structures and Compliance**: From LLCs to corporations, I'll guide you through the legal aspects of running a barbershop and staying compliant with local regulations.

14. **Bonus Insights**: I'll share additional lessons, strategies, and stories that didn't fit neatly into the other chapters but are just as valuable.

MY PHILOSOPHY: START SMALL, SCALE SMART

Throughout my entrepreneurial journey, one principle has guided me: start small, scale smart. I've built businesses with as little as $8, proving that you don't need massive investments to achieve great results. By focusing on strategy, creativity, and reinvesting profits, I've consistently turned small beginnings into thriving ventures.

This philosophy is at the heart of Phase Two. You'll see how I applied it to reopen my barbershop and grow it from nothing into a six-figure operation in just two years. It's about working smarter, not harder, and making every dollar and decision count.

A NOTE TO THE READER

This section isn't just about my journey—it's about empowering you to achieve your own success. Whether you're opening your first shop, revitalizing an existing one, or just curious about the process, the lessons in Phase Two are actionable, proven, and designed to inspire.

Let's jump into Chapter 1 and begin this next phase of the journey together. Success is within reach—it's time to make it happen.

Blueprint 1
Why I Jumped Back into the Game

The journey back into barbering after a long hiatus was not something I initially planned. It was inspired by a combination of past experiences, a love for the craft, and a desire to test myself. In this blueprint, I'll take you through three key aspects of my journey: the creation of the Barbershop Cash Flow course, my background in internet marketing and what I did to start over in 2017 and by 2019 has revenue of over $100,000 a year. These elements not only shaped my approach but also reignited my passion for opening another barbershop.

THE CREATION OF THE BARBERSHOP CASH FLOW COURSE

In 2017, I was deep into the world of internet marketing, creating courses and products to generate income online. One of the most rewarding methods in this field is information marketing—teaching others about a topic you know inside and out. With years of barbering experience under my belt, I decided to package that knowledge into a course: **Barbershop Cash Flow.**

The idea was simple: create a membership website with a member area where barbers could learn the strategies I had used to build two successful barbershops in my early years. I began writing down everything I knew—how I opened my first shop, built clientele, managed cash flow, and maximized profits. It was an exciting process, but something unexpected happened while I worked on the course. I started to miss barbering.

The memories of the craft, the hustle, and the satisfaction of running a barbershop began to resurface. I found myself thinking, *Why not try it again? Why not apply these lessons in real time?* A week after launching the course, I approached my wife with the idea of opening another barbershop. She was hesitant at first, reminding me that I had sworn off the industry years ago, but she supported me. That support set everything in motion.

What started as a course became a personal challenge: *Could I take everything I was teaching and prove its effectiveness in today's market?* By February 2017, I decided to find out.

MY HISTORY IN INTERNET MARKETING

After leaving barbering, I discovered the power of the internet. In 2001, I created the *Hustling CD* series, designed to help young people find legal ways to succeed. To market the series, I launched my first website. It was a simple project, but it introduced me to the potential of online business.

LEGAL HUSTLING SERIES

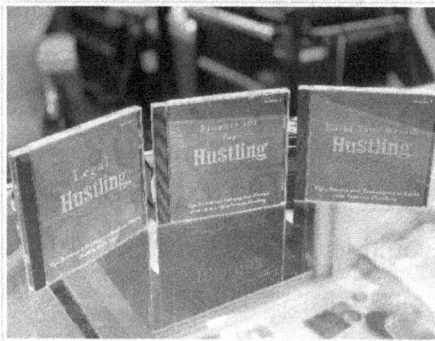

VOLUME 1 ORIGINALLY RELEASED IN 2001
VOLUME 2 AND 3 ORIGINALLY RELEASED IN 2003

Between 2003 and 2005, I immersed myself in learning web programming. Back then, building a website was expensive, and I wanted to cut costs by doing it myself. By 2005, I had mastered the basics of programming and partnered with a music producer to launch an online beat-selling platform. In the first month, the site made

$20,000. That success snowballed into other ventures, including **RocBattle.com**, a website I built for just $8 that went on to generate millions.

By 2017, I was running multiple online businesses, including software development and hosting services for music producers. These ventures allowed me to work from home, but after years of sitting behind a computer, I missed the energy of working with people face-to-face.

WHY I RETURNED TO BARBERING

The idea of opening another barbershop wasn't just about revisiting an old passion—it was about proving to myself that the strategies I taught could still work in today's world. I wanted to show that with the right mindset and approach, you could build a thriving business from scratch.

MASTER BARBER AL

When I launched **Barbershop Cash Flow**, I didn't have a single client. But using the same principles I had developed in the past, I built a successful shop within two years, generating over

$100,000 annually. This phase of my journey is about sharing that experience with you—step by step, blueprint by blueprint.

WHAT'S NEXT?

In the upcoming blueprints, I'll walk you through the exact process I used to reopen a barbershop and turn it into a profitable business. From researching the right location to recruiting barbers and managing daily operations, you'll see how everything I've learned came together in real-time.

The goal is not just to teach you what I did but to inspire you to take action and create your own success story. Let's get started with Blueprint 2.

Blueprint 2
Scouting the Competition and Winning

Before jumping back into the barbering business, I knew I needed to arm myself with as much knowledge as possible about the

Master Barber Al

local market. This blueprint walks you through how I researched the surrounding area, evaluated the competition, and used that information to shape my approach. The goal was to understand the market dynamics and find my place in it.

DECIDING ON AN AREA

When I first considered opening another barbershop, I set a clear boundary for myself: I didn't want to travel more than 15 miles from home. Having a manageable commute was important to me, especially since I was returning to the industry after a long hiatus. My goal was to build a successful business without creating unnecessary stress from long drives or being too far from my established home life.

However, I also kept an open mind. If a golden opportunity presented itself outside my preferred radius, I was willing to consider it. But for the most part, I was focused on finding a location close to home that would allow me to balance work and personal life effectively.

In Monroe County, where I live, the population exceeds 160,000 people—more than enough to support a thriving barbershop. When you consider that even a single barber can succeed with fewer than 1,000 clients, I knew the market was promising. With a population that large, there was plenty of room for a shop like mine to grow.

EVALUATING THE DEMOGRAPHICS

One thing I knew from my past experience was that I preferred a diverse clientele. My first shop was located in a predominantly African-American neighborhood, but my second shop was more multicultural. I found I enjoyed the variety that came with serving clients from different backgrounds, and I wanted to replicate that experience in my new shop.

Monroe County and the Poconos offered the diversity I was looking for. To confirm my assumptions, I used tools like **TownCharts.com** to analyze demographic data, including population breakdowns by age, race, and income levels. This helped me understand the potential client base and ensured that my vision for a multicultural barbershop aligned with the area I was targeting.

VISITING OTHER BARBERSHOPS

Researching the competition was a crucial step. I wanted to understand the local market, including the pricing, services, and overall atmosphere of other shops. I visited four or five barbershops in the area, including one in the mall, and took note of everything.

Pricing

- The mall shop charged $20 per haircut.
- Two shops closer to the mall charged $25 per haircut.
- Another shop in a nearby town charged $18 per haircut.
- One upscale shop charged $30 per haircut.

This gave me a clear picture of the pricing landscape and helped me decide where to position myself in terms of affordability and value.

APPEARANCE AND ATMOSPHERE

I also paid attention to the presentation of each shop. Some were clean, professional, and inviting, while others felt more run-down and unwelcoming. For example, the shop charging $18 for haircuts looked unkempt, while the shops charging $25 and $30 had a more polished appearance.

This was a reminder that presentation matters. Clients are willing to pay more for a shop that looks and feels professional.

Operating Models

Each shop had its own approach to handling clients:

- Two shops relied solely on appointments.
- One shop took walk-ins but only after 4 PM.
- Others combined appointments with walk-ins.

Understanding how other shops managed their flow helped me identify opportunities to differentiate myself. For instance, if most shops were appointment-only, I could stand out by offering a balance of walk-ins and appointments.

UNDERSTANDING BARBER PAY STRUCTURES

I also spoke with barbers and shop owners to learn about the pay structures in the area. This was critical because it helped me understand what I would need to offer to attract barbers to my shop.

- At the mall shop, barbers paid $300 per week in rent but worked in shifts: 9 AM to 3 PM or 3 PM to 9 PM.
- Other shops charged similar weekly rents, around $300, which equates to $1,200 per month.

Hearing these numbers was eye-opening. As I planned my own shop, I knew I needed to offer competitive terms to attract skilled barbers, but I also wanted to ensure those terms were fair and sustainable for my business.

Key Takeaways

Researching the area gave me a wealth of valuable information:
- I confirmed that there was a large, diverse population to support my shop.
- I identified the pricing landscape and decided where I wanted to position myself.
- I evaluated the competition's strengths and weaknesses, giving me insight into how I could stand out.
- I learned what barbers were paying for chair rentals and what I would need to offer to be competitive.

This process wasn't complicated, but it was thorough. By taking the time to visit shops, talk to barbers, and study the market, I gained a clear understanding of the local barbering climate. This knowledge became the foundation for my next steps.

Blueprint 3
Finding the Goldmine Location

Selecting the perfect location for your barbershop is one of the most critical decisions you'll make. It impacts your visibility, accessibility, and overall success. In this blueprint, I'll walk you through my process of choosing a location—from the external factors that influenced my decision to the internal layout and pricing considerations.

WHAT I LOOK FOR IN A LOCATION

When I began my search, I revisited principles I'd outlined in my earlier *Barbershop Cash Flow* course. I also updated these concepts to fit my current circumstances. Here's a breakdown of the key factors I considered:

1. FOOT TRAFFIC

Foot traffic is invaluable. While social media can drive clients, there's no substitute for people walking by your shop and noticing it during their daily routines. In my early shops, I used sandwich boards outside to draw attention. While I didn't rely on this alone, the visibility created by foot traffic brought in consistent business.

Although foot traffic isn't essential, it's highly beneficial for fast growth. A shop located in a high-visibility area requires less marketing to attract walk-ins.

2. PROXIMITY TO TRANSPORTATION

In New York, my first shops were near train and bus lines, which brought in a steady stream of potential customers. For my current shop in the Poconos, there are no train systems, but the local bus line runs right past my shop. Bus stops near traffic lights allow passengers to look around and notice businesses, making this a valuable feature for my location.

3. PROXIMITY TO LANDMARKS

Being near well-known landmarks, such as malls or grocery stores, helps people locate your shop easily. My shop is less than a mile from Walmart and about 2.4 miles from a popular mall. These locations attract a large number of people, some of whom might stumble upon your shop while running errands.

4. RESIDENTIAL COMMUNITIES

It's important to be near apartments, housing developments, or neighborhoods. Shops located on side streets or in isolated areas tend to struggle because they lack a consistent flow of nearby customers. Being part of a thriving community can create a steady client base.

5. TRAFFIC LIGHTS

Stoplights create natural pauses in traffic, giving people a chance to notice your shop. Both of my previous shops were near stoplights, and I often heard from customers that they spotted the shop while waiting at a light. My current shop is near two busy stoplights, which has proven to be a significant advantage.

6. SCHOOLS

Being close to schools can bring in a younger clientele and their families. My shop is within a two-mile radius of several schools, including high schools, elementary schools, and even a college.

These institutions generate consistent traffic, especially during the school year.

7. RESTAURANTS

Restaurants bring people out, especially in the evenings. If your shop is near popular dining spots, people are more likely to notice it. My shop is surrounded by various restaurants, which keeps the area active and helps with visibility.

WHAT I LOOK FOR INSIDE THE SHOP

1. SPACE FOR AT LEAST EIGHT CHAIRS

To build a shop that can grow and scale, I needed enough space to comfortably fit eight chairs and a waiting area. This setup allows me to bring in additional barbers and cover operating expenses while maximizing profitability.

2. A LARGE SHOP WINDOW

A big shop window is a huge plus. It lets people see inside without committing, which makes them more likely to step in. My current shop has a large window, and every day, I see people pause to look inside before deciding to come in. This visibility builds trust and curiosity.

3. AFFORDABLE RENT AND EXPENSES

My goal was to keep rent and expenses under $2,000 per month. This allowed me to operate comfortably, even during slow months. By keeping fixed costs low, I ensured that I could reinvest profits back into the business.

4. ADEQUATE SQUARE FOOTAGE

I aimed for a shop between 900 and 1,500 square feet. This size is ideal for fitting multiple chairs while leaving room for customers to sit comfortably.

EVALUATING AND CHOOSING A LOCATION

As I searched for a location, I evaluated several potential spots. Some looked promising at first but didn't meet all my criteria. Here's how I assessed them:

- **Rejected Locations**: I avoided spaces that lacked visibility, had minimal foot traffic, or were far from residential or commercial hubs.
- **Chosen Location**: My final choice ticked most of the boxes. It had good visibility, affordable rent, proximity to high-traffic landmarks like Walmart, and enough space to grow.

Key Takeaways

Finding the right location isn't just about what looks good on paper. It's about understanding your business needs and how a location will help you meet them. By considering both external and internal factors, I positioned my shop to attract customers and grow quickly.

In **Blueprint 4**, I'll discuss how I set up the shop and managed costs to create a professional, welcoming environment without overspending. See you there.

Blueprint 4
Making the Landlord Work for You

Securing a space for your barbershop is more than just finding the right location—it's about negotiating terms that set your business up for success. In this blueprint, I'll share how I navigated the process of working with a private landlord to secure my shop. I'll compare private versus commercial landlords, outline my negotiation tactics, and detail the key deal points I secured in my lease.

PRIVATE VS. COMMERCIAL LANDLORDS

> *Private Landlords* are those who own a building individually out right and call all the shots. *Commercial Landlords* are properties I would consider own by corporations that usually have multiple buildings and strip malls with a lot more red tape and restrictions

The type of landlord you deal with can significantly impact your experience and costs. Here's how private landlords differ from commercial ones:

Private Landlords

- **Flexibility**: Private landlords tend to be more willing to negotiate terms, especially if the property has been vacant for a while.

- **Lower Fees**: Common area maintenance (CAM) fees, often associated with commercial properties, are usually not part of private lease agreements.

- **Personal Interaction**: You can often communicate directly with the landlord, making it easier to address issues quickly.

- **Greater Value**: Private landlords value tenants who can pay consistently and take care of the property, which can work in your favor during negotiations.

Commercial Landlords

- **Higher Costs**: CAM fees, real estate taxes, and insurance costs are typically passed on to tenants.
- **Structured Processes**: Expect formal procedures and less flexibility, as most commercial properties are managed by larger companies.
- **Impersonal**: Communication often involves property managers rather than the owner, leading to delays in resolving issues.

NEGOTIATION TACTICS

1. **Do Your Research**

   Before meeting the landlord, gather as much information as possible about the property, its history, and the landlord's situation. For instance, I learned that the property I was considering had been vacant for three months, giving me leverage during negotiations.

2. **Ask for What You Want**

   Never hesitate to state what you want clearly and confidently. For example, when the landlord quoted me $1,200 per month, I immediately countered with a lower amount, which led to further discussions and eventual concessions.

3. **Listen to Their Pain Points**

   Pay attention to what the landlord shares about past tenants or challenges with the property. Use this information to position yourself as a reliable tenant who won't repeat those issues.

4. **Take Your Time**

   Never rush into an agreement. I intentionally let a week pass after my initial meeting to give the landlord time to consider my offer. This tactic demonstrated my willingness to walk away if my terms weren't met.

5. **Make it a Two-Way Street**

   Negotiations should involve give-and-take. For instance, I agreed to a minimal parking fee in exchange for a one-year waiver on that expense.

6. **Ease Their Concerns**

   Landlords want to feel confident about their tenants. I assured my landlord of my financial stability and my ability to attract clients, even though I was starting from scratch.

7. **Don't Take It Personally**

   Negotiations can get heated, but it's important to focus on the business side of the conversation. Despite a few disagreements, I maintained a professional demeanor, which ultimately led to a successful agreement.

KEY DEAL POINTS

Here are the major points I secured in my lease agreement:

1. Five-Year Lease with a Five-Year Renewal Option

This term ensured stability for my business while giving me the flexibility to decide whether to renew after five years.

2. First Right of Refusal

This clause allows me to match any offer if the landlord decides to sell the property, ensuring I have the opportunity to secure the building if my business thrives.

3. Waived Real Estate Taxes and CAM Fees

Unlike my first shop, where I paid a portion of real estate taxes, my current lease includes no additional fees beyond the agreed-upon rent.

4. Negotiated Parking and Water Costs

I successfully negotiated free parking for the first year and avoided a flat water fee by demonstrating that my barbershop would use minimal water compared to a salon.

5. Flexible Payment Terms

I convinced the landlord to delay the start of rent payments until my shop opened, giving me time to set up and begin generating income before incurring expenses.

Lessons Learned

1. **Know Your Value**: Understand what you bring to the table as a tenant and use it to your advantage.
2. **Be Willing to Walk Away**: Your willingness to walk away can often lead to better terms.
3. **Secure Your Investment**: Clauses like the first right of refusal protect your business in the long run.
4. **Think Beyond Rent**: Look at the full scope of expenses, including parking, utilities, and potential CAM fees.

FINAL THOUGHTS

Negotiating with a landlord is a critical step in establishing your barbershop. By doing thorough research, listening carefully, and confidently advocating for your needs, you can secure a lease that sets your business up for long-term success.

Blueprint 5
Don't Break the Bank Setting Up Shop

Establishing a barbershop from scratch requires meticulous planning, cost-saving strategies, and a commitment to reinvesting in your business. In this blueprint, I'll share the steps I took to set up my shop, highlighting how I worked within a strict budget, saved costs wherever possible, and built a sustainable business using earned income.

BARBERSHOP BUDGET

My wife and I set a budget of $5,000 for setting up the shop. This excluded rent and security deposit but covered everything from renovations to initial marketing materials. Setting a budget kept us focused and encouraged creativity in cutting costs.

Key Financial Highlights

- **Negotiated Rent**: I secured a favorable lease with a reduced rent, one month free, and a $1,000 deposit.
- **$5,000 Setup Allocation**: Funds were designated for essential items, equipment, and initial marketing.

CUTTING COSTS WITHOUT COMPROMISING QUALITY

1. PLUMBING

The shop didn't have existing plumbing for a barbershop. Instead of hiring expensive professionals, I researched and used **shark bite fittings** to install the plumbing myself. This method saved me thousands, bringing the total plumbing cost to just **$1,300**.

2. PAINT AND DESIGN

- **Materials**: Bought three gallons of $15 paint from Walmart.
- **DIY Work**: I painted the shop myself, adding unique designs to create a premium look. Customers often assumed the shop was high-end due to the professional appearance. Total cost: **$60**.

3. FLOORING

I tackled the flooring myself with my son, using tutorials from YouTube. Materials, including commercial tiles and adhesive, totaled **$600**, saving over $1,000 in installation costs.

4. FURNITURE

- Repurposed folding chairs from my mother's church, cleaning and refurbishing them to look new.
- Purchased minimal furniture initially, focusing on what was necessary to operate.

5. EQUIPMENT

- **Hot Water Heater**: Purchased a small unit for **$300** and installed it myself.
- **Barber Pole**: One of the few new purchases, a $59 pole from Amazon.
- **Miscellaneous Items**: Found great deals on Facebook Marketplace, including a refrigerator for $100 and a $200 TV originally priced at $450.

6. MARKETING MATERIALS

- Ordered **5,000 full-color flyers** for **$90** and business cards to introduce myself to the community.
- Personally distributed flyers at Walmart, aiming to shake hands with at least 10 people per visit. This personal approach brought in many of my first customers.

BUILDING OFF EARNED INCOME

Starting small and reinvesting profits allowed me to expand sustainably without incurring debt.

Steps to Reinvest

1. **Focus on Essentials**: I used the initial profits to cover rent and reinvest in the shop.
2. **Paid Marketing**: Facebook Ads became a major driver of traffic, with campaigns costing as little as **$10 per 1,000 views**.
3. **Gradual Upgrades**: As revenue grew, I improved equipment, furniture, and amenities.

Key Principle: Don't Eat Your Profits

Inspired by biblical teachings, I adhered to the principle of reinvesting the first fruits of my earnings. Instead of spending profits on personal expenses, I put them back into the business, ensuring continuous growth.

LESSONS FROM SETTING UP SHOP

1. **Be Resourceful**: From DIY projects to finding deals online, resourcefulness can save thousands.

2. **Stick to a Budget**: A clear financial plan prevents overspending and encourages smarter decisions.
3. **Reinvest Wisely**: Early profits should go back into the business to ensure long-term success.
4. **Community Engagement Works**: Handing out flyers and meeting people face-to-face created a personal connection that built trust and brought in loyal clients.

FINAL THOUGHTS

Setting up a barbershop is as much about strategy as it is about skill. By starting small, making smart financial decisions, and focusing on earned income, I built a solid foundation for my business.

In **Blueprint 6**, I'll share my launch strategy and pricing approach, including how I positioned my shop to attract a steady stream of clients from day one.

Blueprint 6
My Launch Plan for a Packed Barbershop

Launching a barbershop successfully requires a well-thought-out strategy to establish your brand, attract customers, and build visibility. This blueprint outlines the steps I took to effectively launch my shop and create a foundation for long-term growth.

Chapter Outline
1. Branding Concept
2. Domain Name and Online Presence
3. Free Haircuts for Social Media Content
4. Social Proof: Building Credibility
5. Business Card and Flyer Distribution
6. Social Media Marketing: Facebook and Instagram
7. Google My Business Optimization

1. BRANDING CONCEPT

- **Simplicity is Key**: My shop is called **Pocono Barbers**—a straightforward name that's easy to remember and directly tied to my location and service.
- **Logo Design**: A clean design featuring a Barber blade icon and a two-color theme of **red, black, and white**.
- **Consistency**: These colors were used across all promotional materials, ensuring a cohesive brand image.
- **Pro Tip**: If you're not skilled in design, use affordable services like Fiverr or Upwork to get a professional logo made for $5–$50.

2. DOMAIN NAME AND ONLINE PRESENCE

- **Secured a Domain Name**: Before I signed the lease, I registered **poconobarbers.com** and **poconobarber.com** to ensure brand ownership.
- **Forwarding to Social Media**: Instead of creating a website immediately, I forwarded the domain to my Facebook page. This saved costs and leveraged my social media presence for online inquiries.
- **Future Plans**: A dedicated website for retention programs (e.g., loyalty rewards) can be added as the business grows.

3. FREE HAIRCUTS FOR SOCIAL MEDIA CONTENT

To build trust and attract clients:

- **Offered Free Haircuts**: I provided free cuts in exchange for permission to use their pictures on social media.
- **Social Proof**: These pictures showcased my work, even while I was still sharpening my skills after 15 years out of the industry.
- **Content Creation**: Each picture or video posted was a marketing asset, helping potential clients see the quality of my services.

4. SOCIAL PROOF: BUILDING CREDIBILITY

- **The "Wow Factor"**: Pictures of well-done haircuts are compelling evidence of your skill.
- **Quantity Matters**: The more pictures and videos you post, the more trust you build with potential customers. Aim for **thousands of photos** on your social platforms.

5. BUSINESS CARD AND FLYER DISTRIBUTION

- **Affordable Printing**: I spent $35 for 5,000 business cards and $90 for 5,000 full-color flyers.
- **Design**: Included my picture, my logo, and multiple images of my work for social proof.
- **Personal Touch**: I handed out flyers and cards myself, engaging potential clients directly.
- **Leveraging Help**: I recruited local kids to distribute flyers in exchange for free haircuts.

6. SOCIAL MEDIA MARKETING: FACEBOOK AND INSTAGRAM

- **Start with One Platform**: Focus on mastering a single platform before expanding.
- **Consistent Posting**: Posted 2–4 quality images weekly, showcasing my best work.
- **Boosted Posts**: Used Facebook's boost feature to reach thousands of potential customers for just $5–$10 per post.
- **Instagram Tips**: Use **local hashtags** in addition to industry-specific ones to reach nearby clients. For example, tag local events, schools, and towns.

Recommended App:

- **VideoShop**: A simple video editing app for creating engaging social media content.

7. GOOGLE MY BUSINESS OPTIMIZATION

- **Claim Your Business Listing**: I registered Pocono Barbers with Google My Business.

Key Metrics:

- **2,600 Searches**: People found my shop in Google searches.
- **51 Direction Clicks**: Customers clicked for directions to the shop.
- **146 Calls**: Generated directly from the listing.
- **14,836 Photo Views**: Customers viewed pictures of my work uploaded to Google.
- **Local** SEO Strategy: Google prioritizes local businesses over websites in search results. Optimizing your Google My Business profile is crucial for visibility.

FINAL THOUGHTS

Launching a barbershop successfully is about more than cutting hair—it's about creating a brand, building trust, and consistently engaging with your community. With the strategies outlined here, you can establish a solid foundation for your business and position yourself for long-term growth.

In **Blueprint 7**, I'll break down my pricing strategy, including how I used a $10 introductory haircut offer to create buzz and attract loyal customers.

Blueprint 7
Pricing Strategies That
Maximize Your Profits

When I first opened my barbershop, one of the most critical decisions I had to make was setting the starting price for haircuts. This wasn't just about making money—it was a strategy to grab attention, build a buzz, and attract customers quickly in a competitive market. I wanted to create what I call the "wow factor," and pricing was going to be my secret weapon.

UNDERSTANDING THE MARKET

Before settling on my prices, I did my homework. I drove around and visited other barbershops in the area, researching their price points. I checked platforms like StyleSeat and Booksy to see what local barbers were charging. The average haircut in my area was priced between $20 and $25, depending on the shop and the services offered. This gave me a baseline to work from.

However, I knew I couldn't just match the competition. I was new in town with no established clientele, and I needed a way to stand out. Charging the same as everyone else wouldn't give potential customers any reason to choose me over the barbers they were already loyal to. I needed to be bold.

CREATING THE "WOW FACTOR"

To make a splash, I decided to launch with $10 haircuts—a price point that was half of what everyone else was charging. Initially, my wife thought this was too low, but I explained that the goal wasn't about immediate profits. It was about getting people talking, building trust, and showing the quality of my work.

I put up a $10 haircut sign in the shop window and plastered the price on flyers and social media posts. The reaction was immediate. Customers were intrigued: "Who's giving $10 haircuts around here?" The buzz spread quickly, and people started stopping by, curious to see if the $10 haircuts were any good.

But here's the key to making this work: my $10 haircuts had to look like they were worth $25. If the quality didn't match the presentation, the strategy would fail. I made sure every customer left with a sharp cut that exceeded their expectations.

BUILDING SOCIAL PROOF

Part of the strategy involved leveraging the power of social proof. I printed photos of my haircuts and displayed them in the shop window right under the $10 sign. Customers walking by could see the quality of my work and realize they were getting a deal.

Social media also played a crucial role. I posted every haircut I did, tagging the shop and using local hashtags to draw attention. People started sharing my posts, spreading the word about the $10 cuts. The more photos I posted, the more people came in to see what the hype was about.

THE CUSTOMER EXPERIENCE

The low price wasn't just a gimmick—it was a way to get customers in the door and give me a chance to sell myself. When people came in for a $10 haircut, they saw a clean, professional shop, received excellent service, and left impressed. Many of them paid more than $10, leaving tips because they felt the cut was worth it. Some customers even handed me $20 or $30 without hesitation.

The buzz also caught the attention of other barbers in the area. Some came by to see what I was doing, asking how long I planned to keep the $10 price. Their concern confirmed that my strategy was working—it was making waves in the barbering community and challenging the status quo.

GRADUAL PRICE ADJUSTMENTS

Of course, I couldn't keep the $10 price forever. After the first few months, I started gradually increasing prices. I introduced $15 cuts on most days while keeping the $10 special for Tuesdays and Wednesdays. Later, I adjusted the $10 deal to specific hours, from 12 PM to 5 PM, to encourage mid-day traffic. Eventually, by January 2019, I phased out the $10 cuts entirely.

Each price increase was a smooth transition. Customers who experienced the quality of my work at $10 were willing to pay more.

New customers came in at the higher price points, never knowing about the earlier deals. The shop continued to grow, and I gained the confidence to charge what my services were truly worth.

KEY LESSONS

The launch pricing strategy taught me valuable lessons about business and competition. Starting low doesn't mean undervaluing your work—it's a strategic move to create momentum. By delivering exceptional quality at an unbeatable price, I was able to build trust, establish a customer base, and create a buzz that money can't buy.

This approach might not work for everyone, but for me, it was a game-changer. It allowed me to turn a one-chair operation into a thriving barbershop, all while staying true to my goals and vision. The "wow factor" was real, and it worked.

Blueprint 8
Setting Big Goals for Your Barbershop's Success

When I first opened my barbershop, I knew the importance of setting goals. Goals are more than just targets—they're the backbone of any successful business. Without them, you're just moving in circles, hoping for progress. Goals give you focus, purpose, and direction. They also challenge you, pushing you to evaluate your progress and adjust as needed. That's why I made it a point to clearly define my objectives before I opened the doors.

GETTING STARTED: BUILDING THE FOUNDATION

From the very beginning, I knew that the first months were not about making money but about rebuilding my rhythm. I had been out of the barbering game for 15 years, so my initial focus was sharpening my skills and refining my routine. I set a simple, measurable goal: complete 4–8 haircuts daily, whether paid or free. I didn't care about profits at this stage—I just needed to get back into the groove.

Every day, I treated each haircut as an opportunity to improve my speed and efficiency. I worked to bring my average cut time down to 20–22 minutes. With each haircut, I found myself falling back into a natural rhythm. Like riding a bike, it all started to come back to me. Soon enough, the rust from all those years away from the clippers began to fade.

The shop was new, and so was I—new to the area, with no established clientele. My goal was simple: let people see the value I could offer. I gave free haircuts in exchange for photos, which I used for social media content. This wasn't just about practice—it was about creating social proof. Each photo represented an opportunity for someone to see my work and decide to give my shop a chance.

PROGRESSING TO PAID CUTS

By the second month, my focus shifted. My goal was now to average 6–8 paid cuts daily. I still did the occasional free haircut to keep the momentum going, but I was beginning to see progress. The shop started to feel busier, and I noticed my daily income creeping closer to $100. I was no longer just practicing—I was building a customer base.

As the weeks passed, I saw encouraging signs. My monthly revenue steadily increased: $689 in the first month, $2,260 in the second, and $3,500 by the third. Each day brought new faces into the shop, and I was starting to believe that this vision could become something sustainable.

BREAKING EVEN AND COVERING COSTS

By Month 3, I hit a significant milestone: covering my rent in a single week's revenue. This was huge for me. It meant that the remaining weeks of the month could go toward reinvesting in the shop, expanding my marketing efforts, and, yes, finally taking home some profit.

I remembered the early days when I didn't even worry about making rent—I was just focused on getting back into the rhythm. Now, I was seeing tangible results. The momentum kept building, and by the fourth and fifth months, my revenue reached $4,600 and $5,200, respectively.

SCALING: ADDING A TEAM

While the shop's growth was exciting, I knew I couldn't sustain this pace alone. Customers were beginning to walk out simply

because I couldn't get to them fast enough. I didn't want to rush the hiring process, though. I had a clear vision of the type of barbers I wanted to work with—individuals who would align with the shop's culture and values.

The first barber, Danny, joined me in July, four months after I opened. Shortly after, he referred another barber, and the team began to grow. By the end of the year, I had a solid group of barbers, many of whom are still with me today. Watching the shop transform from a one-chair operation to a fully staffed barbershop was deeply rewarding.

THE POWER OF GOALS

Looking back, I see how vital my goals were to this journey. They gave me a roadmap when I was starting from scratch. Whether it was perfecting my rhythm, growing my customer base, or covering my rent, each goal was a stepping stone to the next level. The key was breaking my objectives into manageable, actionable steps and staying consistent.

For anyone starting out, I can't emphasize enough the importance of setting clear goals. Write them down. Review them regularly. Adjust them as you grow. They will keep you focused and motivated, even when progress feels slow.

As I moved forward, I continued to set new goals—expanding services, increasing revenue, and building a reputation as one of the go-to barbershops in the area. Each goal led to the next, creating a cycle of growth and success. That's the power of setting goals and sticking to them. They turn dreams into reality, one step at a time.

Blueprint 9
Attracting Barbers Who Fit Your Vision

Attracting the right barbers to join my shop was a crucial step in building a successful business. I knew that bringing in the right team could make or break the shop's growth and reputation, so I took a strategic approach to finding and recruiting barbers. This process involved research, offering unique benefits, and creating a consistent message to attract barbers who were not only skilled but also aligned with my vision.

UNDERSTANDING THE MARKET

Before anything else, I conducted thorough research on the local market to understand the standard rates for barbers renting chairs. In my area, most shops operated on a booth rental system, with weekly rates starting at $300 and going even higher for prime locations. For example, the mall just a few miles from my shop charged $305 per week for part-time shifts—morning or evening. Only one shop offered a commission-based system, and one of their barbers eventually joined my team, doubling their income.

This research gave me two key insights:

1. The market was lucrative enough for barbers to make money despite the high rental costs.
2. Offering a more affordable and flexible alternative would make my shop a highly attractive option.

CRAFTING A BETTER OPPORTUNITY

To differentiate my shop, I decided to offer benefits that other shops weren't providing. For instance, I introduced a policy where barbers could take two weeks off per year without having to pay booth rent. This was a simple but effective perk, as most shops required barbers to pay rent regardless of whether they worked. I also started with a much lower weekly booth rent of $125, significantly undercutting the competition while still covering my costs.

I framed this lower rent as an opportunity for barbers to save money—about $400 extra each month compared to other shops. I emphasized how that savings could be used toward car payments, housing, or other priorities. The message resonated with barbers who felt overburdened by high booth rents elsewhere.

PATIENCE IN HIRING

Despite the enticing offer, I didn't rush into hiring just anyone. I was patient and deliberate, waiting for the right barbers who fit the shop's culture and standards. It took five months after opening my doors before I hired my first barber. During that time, I had several inquiries, but I turned away individuals who didn't meet my expectations. This patience paid off, as the barbers I eventually brought on board have been with me for years.

CONSISTENT ADVERTISING

One of my earliest lessons in recruiting came from a seasoned barber who advised me to always keep a "Barbers Wanted" sign visible, even when the shop was fully staffed. Following his advice, I placed a sign in the shop window that simply read, "Barbers Wanted." This small but constant reminder allowed me to collect contacts and build a pipeline of potential recruits. Even though my team has been stable, I'm always prepared for unexpected changes.

Social media also played a significant role in my recruitment strategy. One of my first posts was a simple ad that read:

- "Barbers Wanted: Busy Location in the Poconos. Booth Rent Starts at $125."

To make the shop appear busier, I used Photoshop to duplicate chairs in the shop for the ad. While it wasn't entirely accurate at the time, it conveyed the vision I had for the shop, helping to attract inquiries. I also highlighted benefits like high foot traffic and earning potential, conservatively estimating that barbers could make $1,000 to $1,800 weekly. Over time, every barber who joined my shop surpassed the $1,000 weekly mark.

OVERCOMING INITIAL CHALLENGES

One unexpected hurdle was the perception created by my $10 haircut promotion. While it brought in customers, it also deterred barbers who assumed they couldn't make a decent income at those rates. However, once my first barber, Danny, joined and experienced the high traffic, he quickly realized the potential. In his first week, he made over $1,000, which convinced him—and later others—that the shop was a profitable opportunity despite the initial low prices.

BUILDING A WINNING TEAM

Within months, my strategy paid off. Danny joined in July, followed by another barber named Jeep(JP) shortly after. By August, I had two more barbers on board. These barbers have been with me ever since, with one exception who temporarily left for personal reasons but later returned. My son, who started cutting hair at 16, also became a licensed barber and now works alongside the team, consistently earning over $1,500 weekly.

KEY TAKEAWAYS

Recruiting barbers isn't just about offering the lowest rent—it's about creating a win-win opportunity. By doing my research, emphasizing benefits, and being patient, I was able to attract talented individuals who were committed to growing with the shop. Consistency in advertising, both in the shop and on social media, ensured that I always had a pool of potential hires ready when needed.

Building a team takes time, but with the right approach, it's possible to create a thriving, collaborative environment that benefits everyone involved. This chapter is proof that patience and strategy can turn a one-chair operation into a bustling barbershop with a dedicated team.

Blueprint 10
The Real Booth Rent vs. Commission Strategy

Navigating the decision between booth rent and commission was a pivotal moment in my journey as a barbershop owner. Having worked in the industry since I was a teenager, I'd experienced both models firsthand, and each had its distinct advantages and challenges. In this chapter, I'll walk you through how I transitioned from a commission-based approach in my earlier shops to adopting booth rent in my current one, and why it made sense for my business.

THE COMMISSION MODEL: A HUSTLER'S START

My introduction to the barbering world at 14 came through the commission model. Back then, I worked in a New York barbershop without a license, splitting my earnings with the shop owner. The typical arrangement was 50/50—$5 for me and $5 for the owner on a $10 haircut. If I had a good day, the tips sweetened the deal, but half of every cut went directly to the shop.

Over time, I saw variations of this model:

- **50/50 Split**: Common for beginners or barbers without licenses.
- **60/40 Split**: A more favorable split for barbers with experience or a solid client base.
- **70/30 Split**: Reserved for master barbers or those with significant tenure and a proven reputation.

When I opened my first shop, I kept this structure, rewarding experienced barbers with better splits. The benefit of the commission model is clear: as an owner, your earnings grow alongside the barbers' productivity. If a barber cuts 20 heads in a week, the shop benefits proportionally. In a thriving shop, this can lead to substantial profits.

For example, in my second shop, I was making $10,000 to $15,000 a month. This income came not only from my own chair but also from the commissions I collected from other barbers. It was a lucrative system for an owner willing to put in the effort to maintain a bustling, high-volume shop.

WHY I SWITCHED TO BOOTH RENT

By the time I opened Pocono Barbers in 2017, I faced a different market dynamic. After conducting research in my area—the Poconos—I discovered that nearly every shop operated on a booth rent model. Barbers were paying around $300 per week for a chair, and only one shop offered commission. This meant I couldn't realistically compete for skilled barbers if I insisted on commission. Asking them to split their earnings after they were accustomed to a flat weekly fee would have been a step backward in their eyes.

I realized that to fill my chairs and attract barbers with strong reputations, I needed to adopt the booth rent model. Booth rent offers a predictable, steady income stream for shop owners. Barbers pay a flat fee weekly, regardless of how many cuts they do. While it doesn't have the earning potential of commission in a thriving shop, it has its advantages:

1. **Consistency**: You know exactly how much income to expect from each chair every week.
2. **Lower Overhead**: Barbers handle their own supplies and tools, reducing the owner's financial burden.

3. **Simplicity**: There's no need to track or audit earnings, as the arrangement is straightforward.

SETTING UP MY BOOTH RENT MODEL

I started my first barber at $125 per week, a competitive rate well below the $300 norm in my area. After that, new barbers were brought in at $150, with a gradual increase to $200 as they built their clientele. My son, who started cutting hair under my mentorship, pays a reduced rate, which is a family benefit I'm happy to provide.

This approach allowed me to grow my team while keeping my chairs full. By the time my shop was running at capacity, I was bringing in over $2,000 weekly just from booth rent, in addition to my own earnings. This consistent income allowed me to meet my goals of generating over $100,000 annually while offering my barbers a better deal than they'd find elsewhere.

A STORY OF SUCCESS: ONE BARBER'S JOURNEY

One of the barbers who joined my shop had previously worked at a commission-based shop, paying $400 to $450 weekly. The shop owner ran into legal troubles, and the business became unstable. This barber heard about my shop and made the switch. At first, he didn't have his license, but I encouraged him—like I do all my barbers—to get it. Today, he's licensed, thriving, and earning significantly more under the booth rent model than he ever did with commission.

FINAL THOUGHTS

While commission can be more profitable for owners, it's not always the best fit for every market or shop. Booth rent gave me the flexibility to attract top talent in a competitive environment and provided a steady, reliable income. The decision to switch wasn't easy—I had always believed commission was the superior model—but adapting to the needs of my market allowed my shop to flourish.

Whether you're opening your first shop or looking to refine your business model, understanding the pros and cons of booth rent versus commission is essential. The right choice depends on your market, your barbers, and your long-term goals. For me, the shift to booth rent was the right move, and it continues to serve my business well.

Blueprint 11
Writing Ironclad Barber Agreements

In running a barbershop, one of the most essential tools I've implemented is a **booth rental agreement**. These agreements aren't just paperwork; they're the foundation for establishing clear expectations and maintaining a professional, organized business environment. In this chapter, I'll share why I use booth rental agreements, some of the key provisions they include, and how they've helped my business thrive.

WHY USE BOOTH RENTAL AGREEMENTS?

When barbers join my shop, the first thing we do is sit down to review the booth rental agreement. This ensures that everyone is on the same page about what's expected—from rent payments to professional conduct. Here's why I swear by these agreements:

1. **Clarity and Understanding**: By outlining everything upfront, there's no room for misunderstandings. Barbers know exactly what they're signing up for, and I know what I can expect from them. This eliminates unnecessary disputes.

2. **Professionalism**: Having a formal agreement elevates the professional tone of the shop. Barbers appreciate the structure because many have had bad experiences in less organized environments.

3. **Conflict Resolution**: If issues arise, the agreement serves as a reference point. It outlines conduct, rent policies, and even the termination process, which can be enforced in a court of law if necessary.

179

KEY POINTS IN MY BOOTH RENTAL AGREEMENT

The agreement is detailed, but let me highlight some of the most important sections that keep everything running smoothly:

- **Rent and Schedule**: Barbers are required to work a minimum of five days per week, and rent is due in advance each Saturday. There's also a rotation for days off to ensure walk-in traffic is distributed evenly among all barbers.

- **Promotional Responsibility**: Each barber is responsible for their own promotional materials and tools. This keeps them invested in building their clientele.

- **Cleanliness and Maintenance**: Every barber must maintain the cleanliness of their station and any shared spaces they use, such as sinks or the break area. A $5 weekly fee is pooled to hire a professional cleaner for the shop.

- **Vacation Policy**: Barbers are allowed two non-consecutive weeks of vacation per year without paying rent. However, they must provide two months' notice to avoid scheduling conflicts.

- **Fines and Penalties**: To maintain order, fines are issued for lateness, unclean stations, or other violations. For instance, cursing in the shop carries a $5 fine per word, and barbers with expired licenses face a $40 weekly fine until their paperwork is updated.

- **Non-Compete Clause**: To protect the shop's interests, barbers are prohibited from opening or working in a competing shop within a four-mile radius for three years after leaving.

WHY THESE AGREEMENTS WORK

One example of the agreement's impact is how it encourages professionalism. For instance, I had a situation where a movie

Master Barber Al

playing in the shop had inappropriate language while families were present. Thanks to the agreement's clear rules about conduct and entertainment, I was able to address it immediately. Everyone understood the expectations moving forward.

Another benefit is the structure it provides for new barbers. When someone joins the shop, we review the agreement in detail, and I emphasize the importance of consistency. This is especially helpful for barbers who are just starting out or transitioning from less professional environments.

EVOLVING THE AGREEMENT

I regularly update the agreement to address new challenges or improve shop operations. For example, a recent amendment allows barbers to use their own credit card processors, provided they're approved by management. Another update clarifies how barbers receive 1099 forms to ensure accurate tax reporting.

Each time the agreement is updated, I issue an amendment for barbers to sign. This keeps everyone aligned and ensures the shop continues to run smoothly.

FINAL THOUGHTS

A strong booth rental agreement is more than a set of rules—it's a tool for fostering mutual respect and accountability. It ensures that barbers understand their responsibilities while protecting the shop's interests. Whether you're a shop owner or a barber, having clear agreements in place can make all the difference in creating a thriving, professional environment.

By setting these standards, I've built a shop where barbers feel supported, customers experience consistency, and everyone benefits from a well-run business.

Blueprint 12
Appointments vs. Walk-ins:
The Business Model That Works

In this chapter, I'm breaking down my approach to running a thriving barbershop through a business model centered around **walk-ins and appointments**. I'll explain the philosophy behind my model, the benefits it offers, and how it has shaped my shop into a fast-growing, customer-friendly space.

DEFINING THE BUSINESS MODEL

A business model is essentially the blueprint for how a business operates to serve its customers. For a barbershop, it includes everything from pricing strategies to the services offered and the types of customers targeted. Some shops focus solely on appointments, while others are walk-in only. Many combine the two.

For me, the business model isn't just about services—it's about creating a system that works for my customers and my barbers. My shop combines **first-come, first-serve walk-ins** with **limited appointments,** and this balance has been key to our success.

WHY FIRST-COME, FIRST-SERVE?

The first-come, first-serve model has deep roots in the barbershop tradition. People walk in, sign a list, and wait their turn. It's simple and effective. At my shop, we've refined this system to make it as smooth as possible. For example, if the shop is busy, we enforce sign-ins to keep things orderly. When it's slower, we manage the flow more informally.

Here's why I prefer this approach:

1. **Flexibility for Customers**: Customers don't have to plan ahead or worry about no-shows. When they're ready for a haircut, they can just show up.

2. **Steady Business for Barbers**: Walk-ins provide a consistent flow of customers, ensuring my barbers are always busy. This is especially beneficial for new barbers who are still building a clientele.

3. **Equal Opportunity**: If one barber has a long line, customers often opt to try another. This spreads the workload evenly among all barbers and helps new barbers grow their skills and confidence.

THE CASE AGAINST APPOINTMENTS

While some shops thrive on appointment-based systems, I've found them to be more trouble than they're worth. Here's why:

- **No-Shows and Late Arrivals**: Managing appointments means dealing with customers who don't show up or arrive late, disrupting the entire schedule.
- **Wasted Time**: If a barber finishes early and their next appointment isn't for another 30 minutes, that's lost productivity.
- **Customer Experience**: Appointments can lead to frustration if walk-ins feel like they're being skipped over.

However, I don't rule out appointments entirely. I limit them to weekdays (Monday through Thursday) and require 24-hour advance booking. This keeps weekends open for walk-ins, which are our busiest days.

A BALANCED APPROACH

While walk-ins dominate our system, we do offer **after-hours appointments** for customers with tight schedules. These appointments, available after our official closing time, come with a premium price—usually $40 or more—which compensates barbers for staying late and ensures these slots are worth their time.

CREATING A THRIVING ENVIRONMENT

The walk-in model isn't just about logistics—it's about fostering a community. Here's how it benefits the shop's culture:

1. **A Buzzing Atmosphere**: When customers gather in the shop, they interact, share stories, and enjoy the social aspect of visiting

a barbershop. This creates the classic barbershop vibe that many customers love.

2. **Opportunity for New Barbers**: Walk-ins expose all barbers to potential clients. New barbers don't have to hustle for appointments because the shop's traffic gives them a steady stream of customers.

3. **Encouraging Growth**: One of my newer barbers recently mentioned how much he's grown in just four months. He's gained a solid clientele simply by serving walk-ins, something that would have taken much longer with an appointment-only model.

A MODEL BUILT ON SIMPLICITY

By focusing on walk-ins, we've created a system that benefits everyone. Barbers don't have to stress over managing schedules, and customers know they'll be served in the order they arrive. It's a win-win that keeps the shop running efficiently and profitably.

As I've always said, the right business model is the one that works best for your shop and your customers. This is what works for me, and it might work for you too. But ultimately, every shop owner needs to design a system that aligns with their goals and vision.

Blueprint 13
Managing Your Shop Like a True Professional

Managing a barbershop doesn't have to be complicated, but there are key practices every owner should implement to ensure smooth operations and a professional environment. In this chapter, I'll share my approach to barbershop management, touching on how to effectively manage barbers, customers, and cleanliness.

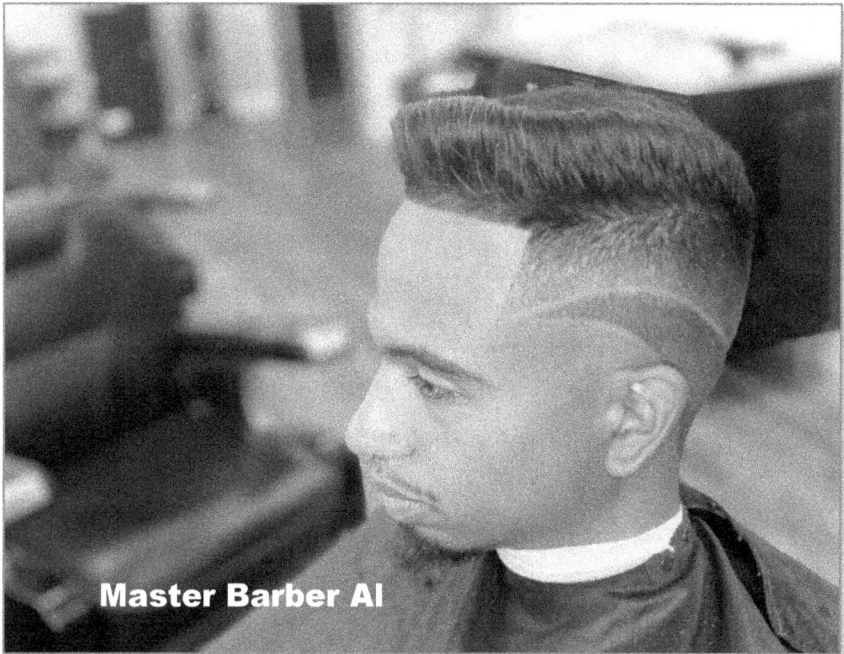

Master Barber Al

MANAGING BARBERS

While barbers in my shop are independent contractors, I don't subscribe to the idea that they can operate entirely as their own bosses. There's a fine balance between independence and maintaining shop standards. Here's how I manage that dynamic:

1. **Schedules and Accountability**:

   Barbers in my shop are required to stick to regular schedules. I've learned the hard way that allowing barbers to come and go as they please creates chaos. Customers lose trust in the shop, and it tarnishes the professional image we strive for. Before hiring a barber, I discuss this expectation in detail. If someone isn't willing to commit to consistent hours, I simply don't bring them on.

2. **Fines for Non-Compliance**:

   To reinforce punctuality, I've implemented a fine system. For example, if a barber is late, they're fined $1 per minute. This adds urgency to their commitments. When I first started, fines were just $5 for lateness, but it wasn't effective—barbers didn't take it seriously. The updated system has made a noticeable difference.

3. **Respect for the Shop's Standards**:

   Every barber agrees to a set of shop rules through the booth rental agreement. This covers everything from professional conduct to dress codes. Having these guidelines upfront eliminates misunderstandings and helps maintain a cohesive environment.

MANAGING CUSTOMERS

Customer satisfaction is at the heart of any successful barbershop. Here's how I ensure a positive experience for everyone who walks through our doors:

1. **Clear Signage**:
   Signs throughout the shop provide clarity on policies and pricing. For example, I have signs stating that customers must return within a certain time after signing in, ensuring fairness for those waiting. This eliminates confusion and creates a smoother flow.

2. **Ease of Payment**:
   We accept cash and credit cards, making transactions as convenient as possible. While cash is preferred, we also have a credit card machine to accommodate customer preferences.

3. **Friendly Atmosphere**:
   Every barber is required to greet customers and thank them when they leave. This simple act of respect creates a welcoming environment and makes customers feel valued. I regularly remind my barbers, "These aren't just customers—they're your money walking through the door."

CLEANLINESS IS NON-NEGOTIABLE

Cleanliness is a reflection of professionalism, and it's something I take seriously.

1. **Daily Cleaning**:
   Barbers are responsible for keeping their stations clean throughout the day and doing a thorough

wipe-down each night. This includes disinfecting tools, chairs, and other surfaces.

2. **Bathroom Checks**:

   A dirty bathroom can ruin a customer's perception of your shop. I check the bathroom multiple times a day to ensure it's presentable. If a customer leaves it messy, it's cleaned immediately to prevent other patrons from encountering it in that state.

3. **Professional Cleaners**:

   In addition to daily upkeep by the barbers, I hire a cleaner to deep-clean the shop regularly. The cost is shared among the barbers through a small weekly fee.

BUILDING A SYSTEM THAT WORKS

Barbershop management is about creating systems that maintain order and professionalism while allowing barbers to thrive. Whether it's setting clear schedules, enforcing rules, or ensuring cleanliness, the goal is to provide a consistent, high-quality experience for customers and barbers alike.

By staying on top of these details, I've been able to create an environment where customers feel welcome and barbers can focus on growing their craft—and their income.

Blueprint 14
Managing Online Reviews – Turning Negatives into Positives

In today's digital world, online reviews play a crucial role in shaping your business's reputation. As a barbershop owner, you'll inevitably encounter negative reviews. This chapter focuses on handling those reviews strategically, turning potential setbacks into opportunities to enhance your reputation.

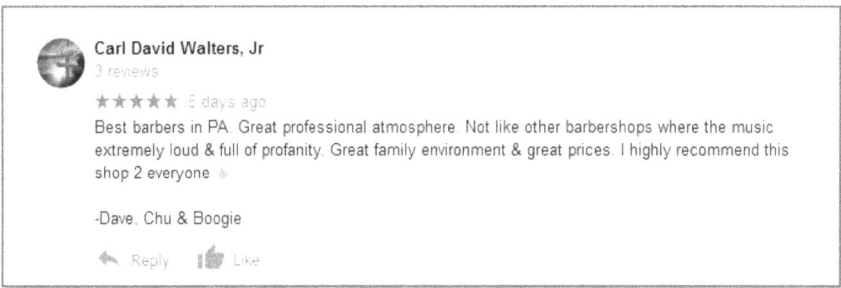

Carl David Walters, Jr
3 reviews

★★★★★ 5 days ago

Best barbers in PA. Great professional atmosphere. Not like other barbershops where the music extremely loud & full of profanity. Great family environment & great prices. I highly recommend this shop 2 everyone

-Dave, Chu & Boogie

↩ Reply 👍 Like

LOCATING THE REVIEWER

When a negative review appears on platforms like Google or Facebook, the first step is identifying the reviewer. Sometimes, their username or full name is displayed, making it easier to track them down. Here's what I do:

1. **Search on Social Media**:
   I typically start by searching for the reviewer's name on Facebook. Most of the time, this works because people in the community are active on social media. If I don't find them there, I move to Instagram. On one occasion, I successfully reached a reviewer through Instagram,

and after a personal conversation, they changed their review from a 4-star to a 5-star.

2. **Message the Reviewer**:
   Once I locate the person, I reach out via Messenger or direct message. While public responses to reviews are important, private conversations are often more effective for resolving issues.

ADDRESSING THE ISSUE

After locating the reviewer, the next step is understanding their complaint. Here's how I approach it:

- **Confirm It's Your Business**:
  Sometimes, reviewers mistakenly associate their experience with the wrong business. For instance, one person left a negative review claiming they had a bad appointment experience at my shop. However, my shop didn't even accept appointments at the time. After a polite exchange, the reviewer realized their mistake, apologized, and removed the review.

- **Listen and Apologize**:
  If the complaint is legitimate, listen attentively and apologize. Even if the issue wasn't entirely your fault, taking responsibility shows professionalism. For example, a customer once complained about her son's Mohawk. After two unsatisfactory visits, she left a negative review. I reached out, offered to personally fix the haircut, and she returned for a third visit. This time, she left satisfied and updated her review.

- **Offer Solutions**:

  If the issue can be fixed, invite the customer back for a complimentary service or offer a refund. However, avoid jumping to financial compensation right away, as it can come across as dismissive. Focus on addressing the root cause first.

REVERSING NEGATIVE REVIEWS

Getting a negative review changed or removed is often possible with the right approach. Here's an example:

A customer left a one-star review claiming my shop was dirty and smelled like urine in the bathroom. After reviewing the video footage, I confirmed the claim was false because they never stepped foot in the bathroom. I reached out to the reviewer privately, explaining how damaging the review could be and highlighting the changes I planned to make based on their feedback. I emphasized my commitment to improving the shop and politely requested that they reconsider the review. After some time, the reviewer responded, apologized, and removed the comment.

WHAT TO AVOID

1. **Arguing Publicly**:

   Never get defensive in public responses. It can escalate the situation and deter potential customers.

2. **Ignoring Reviews**:

   Negative reviews that go unanswered can harm your credibility. Always respond, even if it's just to acknowledge the feedback.

FINAL THOUGHTS

Dealing with negative reviews requires patience and humility. While you won't win over everyone, most people appreciate a business owner who takes the time to address their concerns personally. By turning negative experiences into opportunities for improvement, you can build a stronger, more trusted brand.

Stay tuned for Part 2, where I'll dive deeper into handling reviews on platforms like Facebook and Google, including real-life examples of reviews I've successfully managed—and one I couldn't resolve.

Blueprint 14
Handling Online Reviews – Part 2

In this continuation, we dive deeper into the nuances of online reviews, exploring how to address both positive and negative feedback, with real-life examples from my barbershop. In today's digital era, reviews hold immense power. A single one-star review can significantly impact your ratings, while a five-star review can attract new customers. Let's explore how to handle reviews effectively.

THE IMPORTANCE OF ONLINE REVIEWS

Fifteen years ago, managing customer feedback was simpler. If someone had a bad experience, it rarely went beyond word of mouth. Today, with platforms like Google, Facebook, and Yelp, reviews are public and influential. Many customers have explicitly told me they chose my barbershop based on reviews, proving how critical they are to a business's reputation.

REAL-LIFE EXAMPLES OF REVIEWS

Here are some highlights of reviews we've received and how I've approached them:

1. **The Four-Star Dilemma**
   One reviewer wrote:
   > "This is an excellent business. I had four other barbers exceed my expectations, but I had one bad experience last summer."

   Despite praising the shop and acknowledging great service, they left a four-star review due to one negative experience with a Barber who no longer works for us. While I can't control their decision, I use such reviews as a reminder to maintain consistent quality across all barbers.

2. **Reversing Negative Reviews**

A reviewer claimed our shop was dirty and smelled bad. After identifying and contacting them through Facebook, I politely explained that their experience didn't reflect our standards and requested they reconsider their review. I even pointed out discrepancies, like the fact that they didn't use the restroom during their visit. My humble approach worked—they removed the review.

3. **The Hard-to-Please Client**

One client told me about their conflicts with three previous barbers. Despite my efforts to clarify his preferences and provide a precise cut, he seemed dissatisfied. He left a one-star review, which I couldn't reverse. Sometimes, no matter how much effort you put in, you can't satisfy everyone.

LESSONS LEARNED

1. **Focus on Patterns**:

Most reviews will reflect your shop's overall culture and service. A few outliers shouldn't shake your confidence.

2. **Encourage Feedback**:

When a reviewer gives less than five stars, politely ask what could improve their experience. Many customers appreciate being heard and might even update their reviews.

3. **Acknowledge the Positive**:

Celebrate positive reviews publicly. One customer wrote:

"By far the best barbershop in the Poconos. The owner runs a very professional establishment."

Reviews like this affirm your efforts and reinforce your reputation.

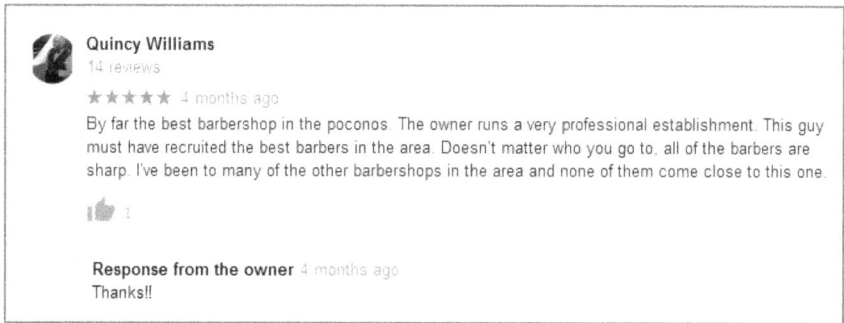

Quincy Williams
14 reviews

★★★★★ 4 months ago

By far the best barbershop in the poconos. The owner runs a very professional establishment. This guy must have recruited the best barbers in the area. Doesn't matter who you go to, all of the barbers are sharp. I've been to many of the other barbershops in the area and none of them come close to this one.

👍 1

Response from the owner 4 months ago
Thanks!!

HOW TO RESPOND TO REVIEWS

1. **For Positive Reviews**:

   - Thank the reviewer for their feedback.
   - Highlight any specific praise they gave to encourage similar behavior from your staff.

2. **For Negative Reviews**:

   - Address the issue calmly and professionally.
   - Offer to fix the problem or provide a free service.
   - Follow up privately to resolve deeper concerns.

FINAL THOUGHTS

Online reviews are a double-edged sword. While they can boost your reputation, they can also harm it. By staying proactive,

197

listening to feedback, and maintaining a professional tone, you can turn even negative reviews into opportunities to showcase your commitment to customer satisfaction.

This concludes Chapter 14 and the course. In future bonus content, I'll cover negotiating strategies, managing equipment purchases, and more. If you have any questions, feel free to reach out. Until next time—peace!

BarberShopCashFlow.com

About the 8-Hour Barber Success Course

I created the ***Barbershop Cash Flow Online Course*** to teach barbers like you how to build a successful barber business and generate six figures a year. In this step-by-step video guide, I share everything I did to grow my shop from scratch and hit $100K annually in less than two years. I've been cutting hair for over 30 years, and I know the challenges barbers face when trying to grow their business. That's why I break down the entire process for you—no fluff, just real strategies that work.

In this course, I show you how I chose the right location and got my shop up and running with very little money. I explain how I packed my barbershop using proven strategies to attract and keep clients while keeping my barbers motivated for long-term success. I also share how I used social media to outshine the competition and built a shop culture that kept customers coming back.

This course doesn't stop there. I teach you how to avoid common mistakes barbers make, negotiate your lease or

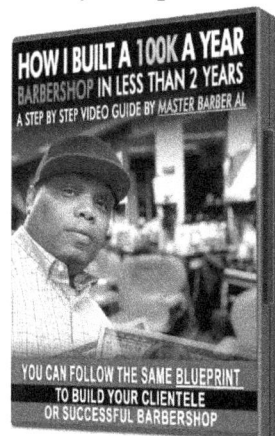

building ownership deal, understand your taxes, and structure your business properly. By the end of the course, you'll have a clear roadmap to open, manage, and grow your own barbershop into a six-figure success, just like I did.

If you're serious about leveling up in the barber business, this course will give you everything you need to get there.

For more information, visit ***BarberShopCashFlow.com***.

What bonuses you get with this online course

To help you build and grow your barber business, I've prepared valuable bonus interviews, audios, and videos with proven strategies and insights. These resources are designed to give you tools, knowledge, and inspiration to maximize your income and success in the barber industry.

Available Now at **BarberShopCashFlow.com**

25-MINUTE AUDIO WITH TODD BROWN

Learn from Master Barber and shop owner Todd Brown, who started cutting hair at 15 and used his barber business profits to invest in real estate. This interview shares actionable steps for achieving success both inside and outside the barber shop.

30-MINUTE AUDIO WITH ROB JONES

Rob Jones, creator of the *FlexRazor* and multi-state barbershop owner, shares his journey. Gain insights into how he built a successful career in barbering while creating his own product and additional income streams.

40-MINUTE AUDIO WITH MARLEY B.

In this interview, Master Barber Marley B. discusses making $300-$400 a day at just 16 years old, opening his own shop, and using advertising strategies to build a strong clientele.

60-MINUTE MINDSET AUDIO BY ALLEN BROWN

Success in the barber industry requires the right mindset and hustle. This audio guides you on how to think and act strategically to grow your barber business.

1-Hour Facebook Marketing Video

In this training video, Master Barber Al shares proven Facebook marketing techniques that helped him grow a six-figure barber shop income. Learn step-by-step strategies to attract more clients using social media.

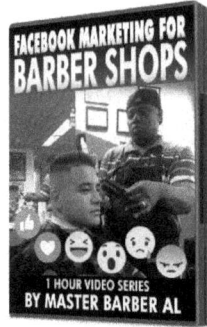

BARBERSHOP TAX TIPS FOR BARBERS

Learn what you need to know about managing your taxes, taking advantage of self-employment benefits, and keeping more of your hard-earned money.

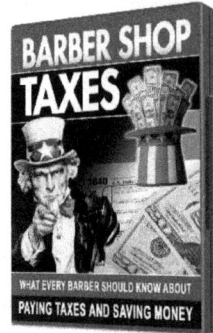

30 TIPS TO INCREASE YOUR CLIENTELE

Explore 30 actionable tips for reaching new clients and expanding your customer base. These strategies will help you connect with potential clients you might otherwise miss.

About Allen Brown

Allen Brown is an accomplished entrepreneur, and dedicated minister with over 35 years of experience in barbering and 25 years in Christian ministry. Allen began his entrepreneurial journey at the age of 14 when he started cutting hair, leading to the ownership of his first barbershop at just 18. By the age of 22, he opened his second shop, establishing himself early as a leader in the barbering industry. In 2017, Allen launched *Pocono Barbers*, a thriving barbershop now operated by his sons. He is a licensed barber in Pennsylvania and New York, as well as a licensed barber teacher in Pennsylvania. Previously, Allen ran *Success Barber Academy, LLC*, where he trained and licensed over 40 students in four years.

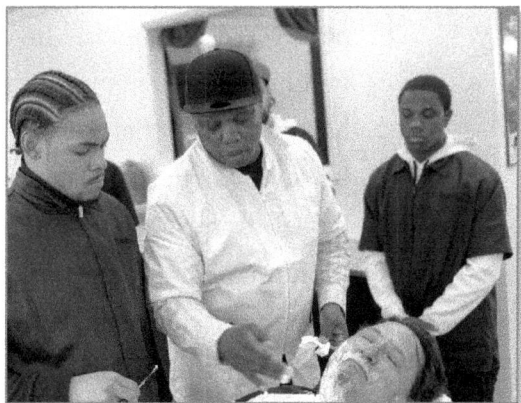

Success Barber Academy

Allen's entrepreneurial reach extends beyond barbering. As a successful internet entrepreneur, he has generated significant income and built a legacy rooted in innovation, hard work, and determination. Alongside his business ventures, Allen's ministry journey began on Easter morning in 1998, and he committed fully to the call in 1999. Over the years, he has uplifted believers through teaching, outreach, and motivational speaking, equipping others with biblical principles for success.

Allen is also the founder of *Build Our Kingdom Publishing*, a company dedicated to producing Christian and business-based books that inspire individuals to align with their purpose. As a published author of multiple transformative works, Allen shares wisdom drawn from his entrepreneurial success, ministry, and life experiences.

Married to his wife Melissa for 27 years, Allen is the proud

father of four young adult sons. Together, the Brown family exemplifies faith, perseverance, and love, building a foundation that honors God, family, and legacy. Whether behind the barber chair, in the pulpit, or as an author and speaker, Allen's mission remains the same: to empower individuals to thrive spiritually, financially, and personally.

About Build Our Kingdom Publishing

BUILD OUR KINGDOM PUBLISHING

— BUILD OUR KINGDOM.COM —

WE ARE A CHRISTIAN BOOK PUBLISHER WITH THE FOCUS ON PUBLISHING NON-FICTION LITERATURE TO EDIFY AND BUILD THE KINGDOM OF GOD.

OUR VISION IS TO SEE PEOPLE COME TO JESUS CHRIST AS A RESULT OF THE TITLES WE RELEASE.

FOR MORE BOOKS BY ALLEN BROWN
VISIT BUILDOURKINGDOM.COM

Million Dollar Seed
How My Last $17,600
Grew to Millions God's Way

"Million Dollar Seed" tells the extraordinary journey of faith, obedience, and divine intervention that transformed the author's final $17,600 into a thriving financial and spiritual breakthrough. This inspiring narrative goes beyond material success, exploring the profound impact of trusting God's guidance in the face of uncertainty.

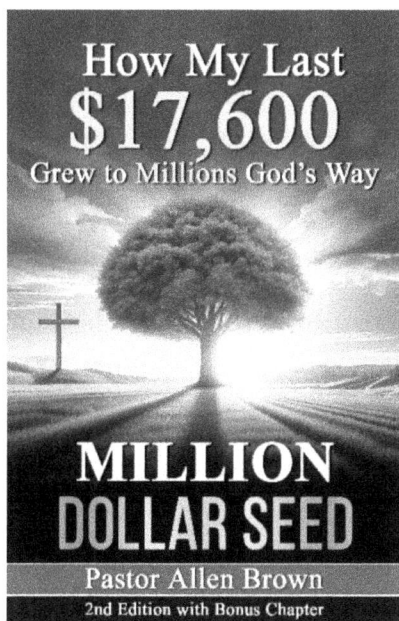

The author shares candid reflections on challenges that tested and strengthened his faith. Paralleling his experiences with biblical figures like Abraham, the story highlights the timeless principles of faith and obedience in unlocking God's blessings.

Structured around three pivotal phases—life before Christ, awakening faith, and a deep trust in God—the book provides a roadmap for spiritual growth and personal transformation. More than a financial success story, "Million Dollar Seed" reveals the deeper wealth found in peace, joy, and alignment with God's purpose.

A source of motivation and practical wisdom, this book invites readers to trust in God's plan, persevere through challenges, and embrace the limitless possibilities of divine guidance.

I Will Teach You How to Hear God's Voice

In a world filled with distractions, hearing God's voice can feel elusive. Yet, the opportunity to connect with the Divine is closer than you think.

In *I Will Teach You How to Hear God's Voice,* Allen Brown draws from his own profound experiences to illuminate the path to divine communication. Through compelling personal stories and biblical wisdom, Allen unveils the life-changing power of hearing and following God's voice in every area— family, business, finances, and ministry.

This guidebook dismantles doubts and affirms that God yearns to communicate with you, guiding you toward your unique purpose. Packed with practical exercises and spiritual insights, it equips readers to cultivate sensitivity to God's whispers, interpret His silence, and deepen trust and faith.

More than a book, this is an invitation to discover a relationship with God that transforms your life. Let His voice be your guiding light.

The Christian Entrepreneur's Compass Volume 1

33 Biblical Strategies for Growing Your Business

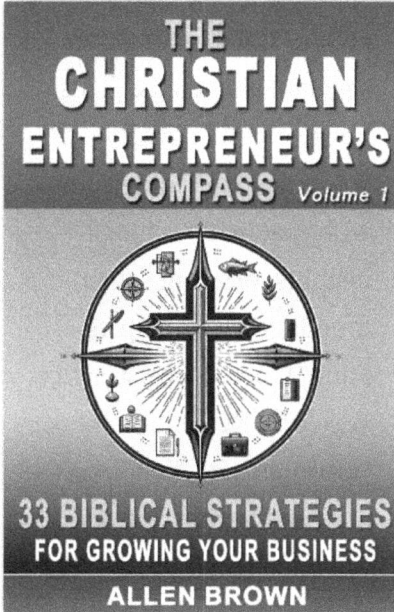

"The Christian Entrepreneur's Compass Volume 1" by Pastor Allen Brown offers 33 powerful strategies to help entrepreneurs align their businesses with biblical principles. Drawing from timeless lessons in Scripture, Pastor Brown highlights stories of figures like Isaac, Jacob, and Joseph, transforming their experiences into actionable insights for modern business challenges.

This guide provides a unique blend of faith and practicality, encouraging readers to balance profit with purpose while building ethical, God-centered businesses. Each chapter delivers wisdom and tools to navigate today's marketplace with integrity and spiritual growth at the forefront.

Perfect for entrepreneurs, leaders, and professionals seeking to integrate their faith into their work, this book serves as a roadmap to lasting success. Whether starting a new venture or enhancing an existing one, "The Christian Entrepreneur's Compass Volume 1" inspires readers to achieve business goals while fulfilling their divine purpose.

Escape the Rat Race:
God's Way

ESCAPE THE RAT RACE
GOD'S WAY

DISCOVER BIBLICAL SECRETS THAT CAN
UNLOCK YOUR PATH TO FINANCIAL FREEDOM

Pastor Allen Brown

"Escape the Rat Race: God's Way" reveals a divine path to financial freedom and spiritual abundance. This transformative guide combines biblical wisdom with practical financial insights, offering seven foundational principles— Faith, Obedience, Sacrifice, Wisdom, Resourcefulness, Gratitude, and Generosity— that lead to true prosperity as ordained by God.

More than a financial manual, this book is a roadmap to a life of purpose, fulfillment, and impact. Each chapter weaves practical advice with spiritual truths, making it accessible to anyone seeking a deeper understanding of wealth and success. It challenges conventional ideas of prosperity and invites readers to embrace spiritual richness alongside material abundance.

Whether trapped in the monotony of daily life or searching for greater meaning, "Escape the Rat Race: God's Way" inspires a shift in priorities. Experience wealth that transforms not just your bank account but your heart and spirit. Start your journey to lasting joy, peace, and divine prosperity today.

The Problem Is You
A Transformational Guide to Self-Discovery and Change

Have you ever felt stuck in your finances, career, relationships, or personal growth—wondering why success and happiness seem just out of reach? The truth might be hard to accept: the biggest obstacle in your life is often staring back at you in the mirror.

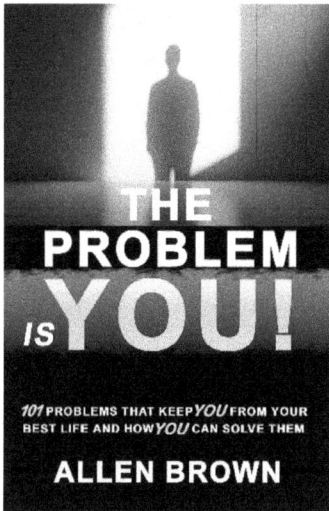

In *The Problem Is You*, you'll uncover the hidden beliefs, habits, fears, and assumptions—the **elements of subconscious influence**—that silently sabotage your progress. Through relatable stories, practical solutions, and powerful biblical insights, this book shows how these unseen forces shape every decision and outcome in your life.

With 101 problems divided into 24 easy-to-navigate categories, *The Problem Is You* helps you identify the blind spots holding you back and empowers you to take control of your success. Whether you're facing challenges in money, relationships, career, or self-worth, this book will equip you with tools to transform your mindset and achieve lasting change.

Your breakthrough starts here.

101 Relationship Problems That Steal Your Joy

101 Relationship Problems That Steal Your Joy offers a powerful guide to overcoming the challenges that hinder joy in your relationships. Whether you're single or in a relationship, this book addresses the problems that create emotional distance, dissatisfaction, and frustration. You'll uncover key issues, such as miscommunication, unrealistic expectations, unhealthy patterns, and the deep-rooted beliefs that prevent connection and happiness.

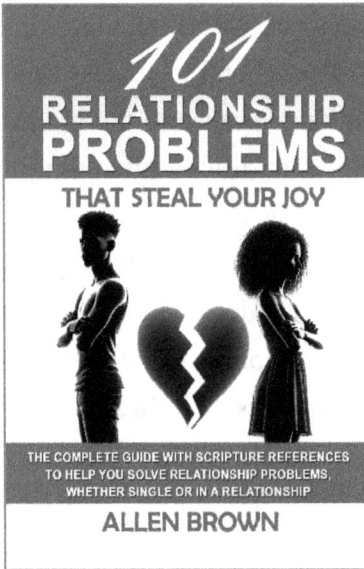

Each problem is explored through real-life examples, subconscious influences, and practical solutions you can start applying immediately. This book empowers you to break free from destructive cycles, build stronger connections, and foster deeper, more fulfilling relationships.

The complete guide provides valuable insights for both individuals and couples, offering actionable steps to reclaim happiness and create the love life you deserve. Don't let unresolved problems stand between you and your fulfillment. Start your journey toward a better, more joyful relationship today!

Your Life Is Not A Coincidence

Your Life Is Not a Coincidence reveals a powerful truth: the events in your life are not random—they are part of a greater design. This transformative book introduces the **3 Pillar Perspective**, a framework that uncovers the hidden forces shaping your reality: **God's Hand**, **Conscious Decisions**, and **Subconscious Influence**.

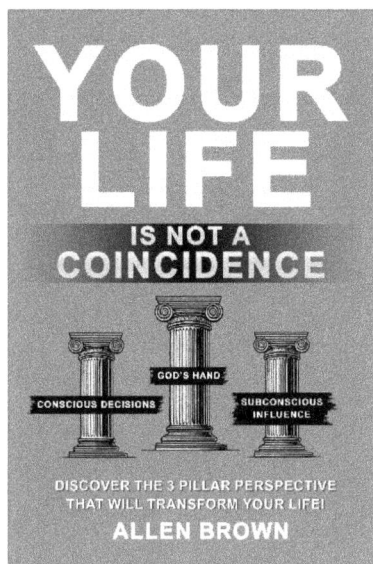

Through personal stories, timeless wisdom, and practical insights, you'll discover how divine guidance, intentional choices, and unseen beliefs work together to create the outcomes you experience. You'll learn to recognize when God is moving in your life, make decisions that align with your purpose, and overcome subconscious patterns holding you back.

This book is your guide to understanding life's deeper meaning and taking control of your future. Nothing is by chance. When you embrace the 3 Pillar Perspective, you'll see that your life is divinely connected, purposeful, and filled with potential.